TALES OF AWAKENING:

A PHENOMENOLOGICAL STUDY OF THE LIVED EXPERIENCE OF COMING TO LIFE AGAIN AFTER A PERIOD OF EMOTIONAL DEADNESS

A dissertation submitted

by

HEIDI M. ELOWITCH (TAYLOR)

to

PACIFICA GRADUATE INSTITUTE

in partial fulfillment of
the requirements for the

degree of

DOCTOR OF PHILOSOPHY

in

CLINICAL PSYCHOLOGY

This dissertation has been
accepted for the faculty of
Pacifica Graduate Institute by:

Lisa Sloan, PhD

Advisor

Diane Gehart, PhD

External Reader

Allen Koehn, DMin

Dissertation Coordinator

FEBRUARY 8, 2010

Tales of Awakening

Copyright: 2010/2017 by Heidi Elowitch (Taylor)

First commercial printing: 2017

ISBN 13: 978-1542596176
ISBN 10: 1542596173

2010: The style used throughout the original dissertation is in accordance with the Publication Manual of the American Psychological Association (5th Edition, 2001, and Pacifica Graduate Institute's Dissertation Handbook (2009–2010).

2017: This manuscript has been reformatted into book form and streamlined for ease of reading and review.

TABLE OF CONTENTS

ABSTRACT

Tales of Awakening: A Phenomenological Study of the Lived
Experience of Coming to Life Again After a Period of Emotional
Deadness

by

Heidi Elowitch

This phenomenological study explored the lived experience of coming to life again after a period of emotional deadness from both an autobiographical-heuristic perspective as well as through participant interviews. The literature review revealed a gap in this area of depth psychology, though work was found in the area of clinical psychology on related general topics such as depression and happiness. The most appropriate supporting literature was found in work on ascent and descent myths, the transformational process of alchemy, and the symbolism in fairy tales. Little was known about the experience from a modern person's view. This study was conducted to explore the phenomenon from the perspective of a current individual who had undergone the ancient heroic journey.

As the researcher, I conducted five face-to-face interviews with two male and three female participants ranging in age from 33 to 47 years old. The participants self-identified as having had the experience of coming to life again after a period of emotional deadness. Using Giorgi's phenomenological method, I analyzed the interviews, found the essential themes, and developed a structural description of the experience. A chapter containing this researcher's own autobiographical-heuristic material was also included.

This researcher found eight common themes that are the essential elements of the topic. They are: Major Trauma, Emotional Deadness, Crisis, Intervention, Painful Awakening, Taking Action, Sharing the Trauma/Telling the Story, and New Life/New Identity. From these themes, this researcher developed a structural description of the experience of coming to life again after a period of emotional deadness.

These results suggest that archetypal human dramas are being lived on and lived forward every day by our friends, neighbors, and ourselves. We may not think of ourselves as Gods and Goddesses; as fighting the curse of the Wicked Queen; or as Inanna, corpse-like and rotting on the meat hook; but these personal accounts testify that this is very much the perceived, lived experience of the participants in this study, heroes in their own right. Clinical psychology needs to hear the cry of depth psychology and shift its focus toward supporting patients in the Underworld rather than simply trying to pull them out.

Acknowledgements

I would like to express gratitude to certain supporters of this research project and to those who supported me personally. Through this process, I learned the validity of the old cliché, "When times are tough, you find out who your real friends are." To that I add, it's a real awakening to find out it's almost no one. So to the few and far between who actually stuck by me through this ordeal, thank you.

Thank you to Michael for loving me the best way you knew how for 5 years. No one comes close to replacing you, and no one ever will. I miss you every day. And sadly, thank you for giving me my topic. I wish you hadn't, but I guess you had to.

Thank you to my father and grandmother for 40 years of emotional and financial support towards this endeavor. I could not have done this without you. I hope you are proud of the outcome.

Thank you to my participants for actively taking the time and initiative to share your personal information so I could graduate and together we could try to help others suffer less. You are remarkable, and I wish I could give you public accolades, but alas, for the best, I cannot.

Thank you to my dearly beloved Taz and Sampson, who were with me day in and day out the years of dying. You were precious, loving, loyal, faithful, funny, and the most adored and cherished guardians a living dying girl ever had. Having to give you up broke my heart and I know it was bitter repayment for the precious care you took of me. It is a wound that will never heal.

Thank you to Takadashi and Rufus. You showed me that it is possible to love again even though you cannot "replace" the originals. I didn't think my heart would work after losing my boys, but it did for you two, and you kept me company through this long and lonely process just like they did. Every day I am overcome anew with the amount of love I feel for you, the joy you bring me simply by being yourselves, and the amount of comfort you add to my life.

Thank you to my committee for believing I somehow had the capacity to finish this in a decent fashion when I didn't believe I would ever live to see the day. Thank you for your feedback and recommendations, and for hanging in there with me when I wasn't sure I could keep holding on.

Thank you to the disciplines of the martial arts and yoga, for allowing me to be in my body when I had to get out of my head and for giving me something to feel strong and confident about when this wasn't it.

Thank you to the therapists I have worked with over the years: Ron, Susie, Brenda, and Lynn—you have each helped me through some very rough times and helped me to understand myself better along the way.

Thank you to my dog walker and lovely friend Carla for helping out with the pups, acting at times as my personal assistant/emergency team of one, and listening to my woes. You allowed me chunks of quiet writing time, extra moments of desperately needed sleep, and the ability to get by without any family nearby or a significant other. If only I'd found you sooner.

Thank you to my friend Kerry, who made sure to feed me and get me out of the house on a regular basis, and never forgot my birthday, even when I wanted to forget it myself. A more devoted, thoughtful, and generous woman would be hard to find. You helped make it all bearable and even enjoyable sometimes.

Thank you to Neal Tubi, computer technician extraordinaire, who miraculously restored my dissertation after a virus removed it from my laptop and corrupted it on my backup flash drive, right as I approached the 200-page mark at the end of the draft. Yes I ran anti-virus software every day. I heard Coyote laughing uproariously as I found only the 1 KB short cut to my 500 KB document and a back-up drive that wouldn't open. I lost my mind for 3 days before I admitted defeat and started calling professionals. Neal had the good sense to be the one to answer his phone, and a mere 4 hours later, Coyote wasn't laughing but neither was I. It was all simply too much for me. You saved the day, Neal, and your compassion, patience, and skills are top-notch.

Thank you to my old-school homeboys and homegirls: Adam, Brent, Candy, and Cherise for being there for me since we were little kids on the street until right now.

Thank you to my girlfriends Jane and Heather for being two of the very few people who cared enough about my dying to bother doing something proactive about it.

Thank you to those who didn't make it out alive: Mike L., Jacquie A., David A, Kirk B., Jacinda J, Eagle . . . see you all someday.

Thank you to Kim, Erin, Samantha, and G for your courage, support, friendship, and examples of kind spirit.

Thank you to Dan and Don for the writing space, flash drive, and family.

Thank you to Mark D. Robinson for assistance with many things large and small and weathering quite a few emotional breakdowns as the defense date grew near.

Thank you to my extraordinary, kind, patient, brilliant, supportive, understanding, nurturing, gentle, expeditious, and talented editor Jan Freya, without whom this project would have been insurmountable. Beyond top-notch editing and proofreading, Jan was part coach, therapist, cheerleader, and friend. I am honored to have had her grace my efforts with her Midas touch.

Finally, thank you to anyone anywhere who has lived through this experience, because it is one hard road to travel and it takes guts not to check out.

CHAPTER 1

INTRODUCTION AND REVIEW OF THE LITERATURE

Introduction

Despite years of research, depression remains the most common psychiatric disorder in North America today, and recovery rates remain less than desirable. The causes of depression and the process of recovery remain unclear. . . .

Although recovery is said to be the vision that should guide intervention in mental health care, as a phenomenon, recovery is poorly understood. (Anthony, as cited in Schreiber, 1998, pp. 269-270)

The word mood derives from the German Mut, which means spirit or soul.

The word disorder derives from the old French word desordere meaning out of line, chaotic. So, mood disorder literally means chaos of the soul. The implications of this go far beyond the medical model's view of illness. What is chaos of one's soul? To answer this question requires entry into the archetypal world of the imaginal, and invokes a spirit of poetic reverie. (Kiehl, 2005, "Pathologizing Depression," para. 6)

It is well known that grief, bereavement, trauma, and depression can be so severe that one becomes hopelessly lost and entangled in their grip, to the point of having disturbed functioning, at best, or committing suicide, at worst (American Psychiatric Association [APA], 2000, pp. 349-351). What, then, allows some individuals to journey so far down into this realm of blackness, or "emotional deadness," yet somehow to find their way out into the sunlight, or "come back to life," once more?

This question of the transitional shift has more than one answer, for the answer is as individual as the people who make the journey. Like many things in life, what works well for one person may not work well for another, and what works effectively for someone at a given point in time may prove fruitless later on. The journey to wellness is not a neatly traveled, linear route but, instead, is circuitous, tumultuous, and unique. As Chalquist (2004) explains, "All minds, all lives, are ultimately embedded in some sort of myth-making. Mythology is not a series of old explanations for natural events; it is rather the richness and wisdom of humanity played out in a wondrous symbolical storytelling. No story, no myth, and no humanness either" (para. 4). For those who suffer in the grip of emotional deadness, no tidily packaged prescription exists to alleviate their condition and bring about swift relief, for emotional deadness is a place beyond depression, where one is cutoff from life.

Autobiographical Origins of the Researcher's

Tales of Awakening

Interest in the Topic

These questions intrigue me for many reasons. The state of emotional deadness is extremely personal to me, for I have lived it. Along with my own experience, people close to me have suffered from it, some of whom have emerged from despair. One very important person did not make it back. This question therefore haunts me and remains unanswered, to a large extent. Most of my friends, acquaintances, clients, colleagues, and relatives have lived through tragic events such as chronic and acute pain and illness, divorce, loss of a spouse or other relative, infertility, or other traumas, yet with time, healing occurred, and they managed to move from their emotionally deadened states to go on and enjoy life once more.

I have endured more than most human beings should survive in one lifetime, and I have come through these experiences not only surprisingly intact but oddly happy. I am interested in the healing element that allows for the transformation from despair to hope and joy. It is likely to be something slightly similar in quality and also unique and personal as actually experienced by each individual; however, each person experiences some transformational shift, and this is what I have sought to give voice to in my dissertation. I am absolutely fascinated with what prompts the healing urge, with the elements of the transformational process itself, with the perceived experience of each participant, with the truism of the cliché, "Whatever doesn't kill you makes you stronger," and with the ways one is, literally, an Other after the emergence from the transformational process. This transformation is nothing short of an alchemical miracle.

Organization of the Study

This dissertation presents a review of literature that explores the myths of descent and ascent from a depth psychological perspective (Chalquist, 2004). Mythological stories describing journeys to the Underworld, the transformational process therein, and the eventual rise to the Upperworld are used to underscore phenomenological interviews of modern versions of the archetypal tale. The work of Jungian and post-Jungian authors is reviewed in relation to the transformative aspects of the journey of descent and ascent.

According to Chalquist (2004), "personal symptoms, conflicts, and stucknesses contain a mythic or transpersonal/archetypal core that when interpreted can reintroduce the client to the *meaning* of his struggles" (para. 4). Working through my own symptoms, conflicts, and stucknesses, I lived an ancient archetypal myth. I had no idea that I had lived through a myth until I began to look at what happened to me from a depth perspective. The course of my return from the Underworld felt incredibly slow, tedious, intricate, and complex, and was interwoven with so many factors it was difficult to separate them. Yet that is what I have sought to do with this dissertation: incorporate my own account of the lived experience of the phenomena along with those of five self-identified "Returned" participants' phenomenological interviews (Giorgi, 1985) about their personal experiences of going into, being inside, and emerging out of the Underworld and returning to life again. The data from my account and these interviews is analyzed using Amadeo Giorgi's (1985) phenomenological method. Jungian, archetypal, and mythological concepts structure the presentation of individual "geographies of return" (D. Sharpe, personal communication, March 14, 2004). My interest was in identifying key elements that mark the turning point when suffering individuals begin to ascend out of the underworld of emotional deadness to live above ground once more, with another chance to drink in the daylight.

Relevance of the Topic for Clinical Psychology

This topic is relevant to clinical psychology because major depression, a key component of my definition of emotional deadness, is an ongoing, serious mental health concern affecting many people (DSM, 2000, pp. 355-356). Depression can be mild to moderate, but always involves some measure of sadness or anhedonia (loss of pleasure in nearly all activities) and disruptions in sleep, appetite, mood, pain perception, and relationships (pp. 349-352). It can present in intensities ranging from mild (i.e., dysthymia) to severe, and it can be fatal, resulting in the loss of one's life, literal as well as figurative (pp. 349-351). The particular focus of this study is on depression as a so-called "living death" or "emotional deadness," which, though presumably less painful for those surrounding the sufferers than actual death, no doubt causes tremendous damage to both the carriers of the state and those that care for them.

For clinicians, depression or emotional deadness can be difficult to treat because much of society expects that doctors can provide a "quick fix," cure problems in one session, and help people feel better right away (Flora, 2006). What about the times when that rapid respite cannot be provided? Moreover, what about those times when therapists themselves fall headfirst into the pit of despair and lose their way? What happens when they lose faith in their foundation, beliefs, courage, and confidence that everything they have studied, absorbed, and upheld as "the way" can actually contain them until they heal? What becomes of them then?

The more that is known about this condition from the inside out, the deeper the examination of every facet of its hold on its victims, the more effective therapists are likely to be. By providing phenomenological descriptions of the transformational aspects that propel individuals from the Underworld to the Upperworld, this study can be of use to therapists in helping their clients recognize these turning points and finding meaning in all aspects of their experience.

Literature Review

Tales of Awakening

Literature Relevant to the Researcher's Theoretical Approach

There appears to be a major dearth of literature on the precise topic proposed for this dissertation—the moment of transformation or emergence from depression to happiness—a void which in and of itself gives weight to the importance of adding to this area of research. There are, however, many related findings of interest well worth noting. Myths and fairy tales have contributed a rich background through which to explore and examine the concept of coming back to life again after a period of emotional deadness, although it is described differently according to the various stories and fables.

Jungian archetypal psychology has fostered a wealth of literature that relates mythological themes, stories, and imagery to the dynamics of the psyche. For the purposes of this study, the work of Jungian analysts and writers is used to explore the archetypal relevance of tales, myth, and legends to the topic of the descent of the psyche into the depths of depression and the transformative aspects of this state that allow for the ascent into new life. Included in this review is a brief overview of how processing death can be a form of transition and healing for both the dead who move on and the mourners who are left behind.

Jungian Psychology

Jungian psychology is part of the foundation of depth or analytical psychology (Chalquist, 2004). It is the body of work originating from the Swiss psychiatrist Carl Jung and furthered by those following in his footsteps. It has some similarities with but also major differences from Freudian theory. Its main goal is to apprehend and integrate deep forces and underlying motivations for human behavior and actions by studying the importance of the phenomenology surrounding dreams, symbols, and mythology (Bothamley, 2002, p. 290). Depth theory is the body of psychology proposed by the Austrian founder of psychoanalysis Sigmund Freud. It refers to any psychology that postulates dynamic psychic (mental) activities that are unconscious. It embraces all schools deriving from Freud, including many that depart widely from his teaching (Bothamley, 2002, p. 143). Archetypal psychology is based on the belief that primordial images reside in the collective imagination of a people, and are expressed in myths and in the figurative dimension of literature (p. 30). Both look to the unconscious mind as the source of growth and healing potential in an individual (Chalquist, 2004).

A central goal of Jungian psychology is the meeting of the individual's life with the world of the supra-personal archetypes through one's encounter with the unconscious (Chalquist, 2004). The unconscious is experienced symbolically through dreams, art, religion, relationships, and life endeavors. Learning the language of symbolism is central to the entire process of exploring the terrain of the unconscious and the realm of the archetypal (Chalquist, 2004).

Tales of Awakening

In Jungian theory, *neurosis* is "a psychological crisis due to a state of disunity with oneself, or, more formally, a mild dissociation of the personality due to the activation of the complexes" (Sharp, 1991, "Neurosis," para. 1). Psychotherapy attempts to reestablish a balanced relationship with the unconscious; being neither overwhelmed by it (psychosis) nor cut off from it (narcissism). The encounter between the conscious mind and the symbolism arising from the unconscious create a rich life and spur psychological development. Jung called this maturational process *individuation* and considered it critical not only to the individual but to society as a whole. For one to transform through the individuation process, one must be open to realms beyond one's ego, including dreams, religion, and spirituality, as well as being willing to question the dominant beliefs and views in the world instead of just passively accepting them (Sharp, 1991).

The unconscious. Jung considered the personal unconscious to be the most critical part of the human psyche (Sharp, 1991). Wholeness occurs through good communication between the conscious and unconscious parts of the psyche. Jung believed that dreams give insight into one's ideas, beliefs, and feelings which are normally out of one's awareness but need to be brought to recognition, and that this material is expressed in a personal vocabulary of metaphorical pictures contained in the unconscious. The collective unconscious contains archetypes common to all humans; therefore, individuation may bring forth symbols that do not directly relate to the life experiences of just one person but rather of the overarching experiences of humanity as a whole: life, death, fear, happiness, and so on. These great experiences may then be integrated into the personality as part of one's growth (Sharp, 1991).

The collective unconscious. The archetypes of the collective unconscious are the underlying roots of the psyche (Sharp, 1991). They are the common psychological lineage and heritage shared by all humanity. They are one's innate predispositions which can be revealed through symbolic forms of communication such as dreams, art, myth, religion, and the ritualistic ways in which humans behave and relate to one another. Jung's theory postulated that the collective unconscious existed across cultures, times, and peoples (Sharp, 1991).

The archetypes. Jung's theory advanced the use of archetypes as inborn, universal templates for thoughts, and he believed they could be used to interpret observations (Sharp, 1991). A group of memories and associations belonging to an archetype is a complex. Jung treated the archetypes as evolutionary processes similar to physical development over time (Sharp, 1991).

Self-realization and neuroticism. The inborn need for self-realization is what drives individuals to process and metabolize these otherwise rejected materials (Sharp, 1991). Jung considered this maturational drive of individuation the natural process of becoming a whole person. Jung postulated that the first half of life is spent distancing from the world in order to individuate and develop a sense of community and spiritual identity. The second half of life is spent reintegrating with the world and joining in the collective identity, focusing on conscious and unconscious feelings. Jung theorized that the main pull of the collective unconscious and self-realization is toward spirituality. If this growth is stunted, symptoms of neurosis may develop, including phobias, fetishes, and depression (Sharp, 1991).

The shadow. The shadow is an unconscious complex containing the repressed and suppressed aspects of one's conscious self (Zweig & Abrams, 1991, p. xviii). The shadow may be either helpful or harmful. If one only acknowledges positive things about oneself, one's shadow material will likely be destructive. If one judges oneself harshly, one may have positive material in one's shadow. Jung called this the "gold" in the shadow and felt it was of great importance for one's shadow to be made conscious and integrated into awareness rather than risk being projected onto others. In dreams, the shadow frequently appears as a dark figure the same gender as the dreamer. Jung's theory states that one deals with the shadow through denial, projection, integration, or transmutation (Sharp, 1991).

Anima and animus. In Jung's theory, the anima is the unconscious feminine component of men, and the animus is the unconscious masculine component of women. Modern Jungian analysts, however, believe that both processes exist in both genders (Sharp, 1991). According to Jung, the anima and the animus behave as guides to the unconscious self, and developing conscious awareness and integration of them is crucial for growth. As with the shadow, an anima or animus that is ignored may be projected onto others and create difficulty in relationships and gender roles (Sharp, 1991).

Psychoanalysis. Analysis is one way to experience and explore unknown material. It is a way to create meaning out of events, symptoms, and behavior in order to gain self-knowledge (Sharp, 1991). Analysis can include dreams, art, poetry, music, and other creative works. Jungian analysts are open to whatever the unconscious may contain and do not hold fixed notions about what must exist (Sharp, 1991).

The complex. Jung appeared to view complexes as somewhat autonomous parts of psychological life. He viewed a complex as accumulating around an archetype (Sharp, 1991). Jung believed that all of human psychological life is based on experiences common to all humanity out of which central guiding complexes are formed, such as the "hero complex," one who separates from the community and conquers some obstacle or struggle which furthers the individual or humanity in some way (Sharp, 1991).

Jung's View of Depression

Tales of Awakening

In Jungian theory, depression is a psychological state characterized by a lack of energy (Sharp, 1991). Energy unavailable to consciousness does not simply disappear. It regresses and stirs up unconscious contents such as fantasies, memories, and wishes that, for the sake of psychological health, need to be recognized and dealt with.

Depression should therefore be regarded as an unconscious compensation whose content must be made conscious if it is to be fully effective. This can only be done by consciously regressing along with the depressive tendency and integrating the memories so activated into the conscious mind—which was what the depression was aiming at in the first place. . . .

Depression is not necessarily pathological. It often foreshadows a renewal of the personality or a burst of creative activity. There are moments in human life when a new page is turned. New interests and tendencies appear which have hitherto received no attention, or there is a sudden change of personality (a so-called mutation of character). During the incubation period of such a change we can often observe a loss of conscious energy: the new development has drawn off the energy it needs from consciousness. This lowering of energy can be seen most clearly before the onset of certain psychoses and also in the empty stillness which precedes creative work. (Jung, as cited in New York Association for Analytical Psychology, 2008, "Depression," paras. 2-3)

Heidi Elowitch (Taylor)

Jung did not necessarily view depression as a mental illness, the way it is often viewed now (DSM, 2000, pp. 345-348; Sharp, 1991). Jung felt that depression could be seen in a much broader way, including a time to rest and regain strength after becoming drained of energy, particularly psychic energy, on multiple levels. "The psyche may cause an individual to slow down into a state of depression for purposes of internal regeneration. A bout of depression can also be a sign that it is time to reevaluate one's life and priorities" (Matsakis, 2008, para. 1). Depressed individuals tend to withdraw from the world and other people and may lack the desire or drive to participate in regular activities. This is often viewed as a negative sign of depression, as something one must be pulled or lifted out of, but Jung believed this inward focusing of psychic energy onto oneself rather than the external world was a time of both retreat and growth as well as a normal phase of the grieving process, not only for the loss of a loved object but for lost or undeveloped parts of the self. In this light, depression, rather than being a negative, is seen instead as one way for "underdeveloped, suppressed, or entirely new longings to assert themselves" (para. 6).

Post-Jungians' Views of Depression

A growing body of post-Jungian research suggests that depression can be looked at as a type of "creative isolation" leading to productive introspection, the discovery of new strengths, abilities, potentials, and new sources of joy and purposeful direction. Suffering signs of depression may be a calling to explore spiritual issues, a need for rebellion of some sort, a call for balance, rest, social contact, free time, recreational or artistic ventures, or a reassessment of one's life until this moment (Matsakis, 2008, para. 7).

Depression can become difficult when it leads to painful rumination, despair, low self-esteem, panic, fear, loss of confidence, a sense of hopelessness, helplessness, despondency, pessimism, anxiety, and impairment leading to suicidal ideation or intent; yet it is precisely this type of depressive crisis that can paradoxically spur new awakenings. One delves into the depths of one's blackest soul moments, finds out one's true nature, and fights one's way back with a new level of awareness and a new arsenal of coping tools. As Mastakis puts it, recent research has found that that even in some instances of trauma or stress-related depression, certain positive personality characteristics can emerge. If someone has been raped or been in a war or a fire, everything isn't fine, but that doesn't mean that they didn't acquire certain strengths or insights as a result of their sufferings. (2008, para. 13)

She goes on to articulate:

Furthermore, the people who report some positive outcome have tended to be those fortunate enough to have had access to some degree of adequate emotional, mental health, and medical support, not those whose health, relationships, or careers were almost entirely devastated by their hardships. In addition, to say that some people have experienced some positive benefits because of their emotional and physical pain doesn't mean they got back everything they lost as a result of their ordeals. They can never be the person they were before they went through whatever injustices or horrors they experienced and some areas of their lives may be permanently scarred by their experiences. In other areas, however, they may have achieved a degree of satisfaction, happiness, and emotional or spiritual growth that might have never been possible had they never suffered to such an extent. (para. 14)

Additional findings in current research (Matsakis, 2008) corroborate Jung's notions that depression is not always a negative that needs to be removed and also give support to certain messages found in ancient Greek myth and in various Biblical, Hindu, and Buddhist teachings: that all events leading to suffering, assuming they do not destroy the entirety of one's inner and outer resources, may well lead to a transformation resulting in greater wisdom as well as a fuller life. The suffering, however, must be intense enough to force one to turn inward for the resources to continue to hold on. Some of the positive outcomes reported by people as a result of having survived severely difficult or painful times include the following:

a greater determination to achieve one's goals; increased self-reliance; the belief that one can cope with difficult situations; a greater self-understanding; increased ability to tolerate and manage uncertainty; increased ability to handle crises; increased awareness of the brevity and fragility of life; greater appreciation for close relationships; increased family and community closeness; increased compassion for, faith in and tolerance of other people; freedom from worrying about death; spiritual growth; increased respect for and ability to manage powerful emotions; and increased capacity for loyalty and commitment. (para. 15)

A Fairy Tale: The Glass Coffin

Seifert (1986) employs the famous fairy tale *Snow White* to explore the phenomena of frozen feelings, inward reflection, feeling as if dead, no longer feeling anything at all, and having life seem to stand still. He describes how individuals who seek psychotherapy for depression can become absolutely horrified, feeling as though life has passed them by, that they have missed out, that they have remained onlookers and spectators rather than active participants. He describes the sensation of patients whereby it seems as though they were waking from the sleep of years, as if a numbness, a spasm, were dissolving, which up until then had blocked and crippled them.

The fairy tale *Snow White* begins in winter, paralleling the bleakness of the soul, and progresses through a conflict, a transition, a transformation, and a new beginning. After the jealous, wicked Queen's attempts to kill Snow White result in putting her into a deep stupor, the glass coffin in which the dwarves have laid Snow White symbolizes being suspended in that stage that is neither living nor dying, but is not experiencing. Seifert describes how patients in this stage of therapy have great clarity of vision for their problems, but are no longer moved by them. They can speak about the most awful suffering with no feeling or affect, for the glass isolates them; they are, in a very real sense, lifeless. He says the glass coffin is an image of a split-off part of the soul, not yet developed and barely alive, but completely known nonetheless. He describes the period of awakening as further developing what is unfinished, making up deficits, setting aside imbalances, and taking care of things postponed. . . . This gives meaningful shape and form to one's life. . . . Old experiences are newly enlivened and become objects of reflection in the present. Old rigidified structures become flexible again or are suffused with new life. The exactitude with which wounded areas are located is impressive, just as is the intensity with which each person desires further development. (p. 7)

With his analysis of the tale of *Snow White*, Seifert portrays a state of numbness and isolation from which one may awaken with new life; however, the work of other writers describes the experience of emotional deadness due to traumatic events as a descent into the underworld, a perspective which utilizes the archetypal imagery and events of myth to explore that state, its transformative aspects, and the ascent from this "living death."

The Mythology of Descent

Smith (1990) discusses the concept of the Underworld as a repository of the archetypal forms of the mind, which give shape and significance to life and art, as a sacred site of initiatory transformation. Smith explains, "The descent to the Underworld cripples the heroic will in order to reveal the poetic basis of consciousness" (p. 29). Smith recognizes and gives voice to the somber but true fact that journeys into darkness force one to give up what one knows and has been able to rely on previously. Such a journey turns people inside out and upside down, and yet, if they survive, they have become open and experienced in ways not formerly thought possible. The weak may become strong, the strong may soften; indeed, the types of transformation are limitless and unknown.

Smith (1990) makes reference to Hillman's discussion of the mythic geography of the Underworld, with its motifs of immobility and passivity, permeated with images of death and illness. Hillman calls the Underworld a place of "blackness, shadows, retardation, mud, bodies of water, revelry, doors and gates, sickness, death, devils, phantoms, shadows, dreams, and the soul" (as cited in Smith, 1990, p. 43). It is a place beyond hope, time, and redemption. Strikingly, Smith makes note of the "intimate relationship between personal collapse and the journey through Hades" (p. 50). Smith finds this dynamic described in the work of novelist D. H. Lawrence as "the process of dying into being, the lapsing of consciousness which is yet the discovery of a deeper consciousness, the dissolution of the hard, intact, ready defined ego" (as cited in Smith, 1990, p. 82).

In fact, an entire body of "Mythologies of Descent" exists in Western culture and is seen as carrying themes and symbols pertinent to the human psyche. They are among the oldest and the most common and are unique in that they symbolically represent death and destruction of the ego and the rise of rebirth and resurrection. In this way, they offer hope and comfort not only on the literal level of the mysteries of life but on the psychological level as well. According to Maggie Macary (2005), studying the mythologies of descent "puts one on a mystical path, searching for initiatory experience which requires a relinquishment of our fragile hold on ego-driven reality" (para. 5). She states that studying the mythologies is akin to entering

> into an imaginal place where Guardians stand ready at the Gates to challenge the courage and commitment of the unprepared or the unworthy. To cross through the Gate, through the threshold of the worlds is to move into a liminal place—a place that is betwixt and between the worlds. Finally, standing before the Other who is death, who is in reality also oneself, one is annihilated into rebirth. (para. 6)

The earliest forms of descent mythology begin with the Sumerian myth of the Descent of Inanna, Queen of Heaven and Earth, into the Underworld to face her dangerous sister Ereshkigal, Queen of the Underworld, to allow for her eventual death and rebirth. "In the Sumerian pantheon" says Macary, "Inanna is associated with the planet Venus, the morning and evening star, whose cycles of appearance and disappearance give rise to tales of a goddess who descends and is reborn" (2005, para. 7). The myth of Persephone and Demeter, she points out, is the Greek recasting of the descent tale, and Christianity recognizes the theme through the resurrection of Jesus.

In modern or postmodern life, psychological, emotional, and spiritual crises not only make one confront physical death as a reality, but also are one's own personal relationship to the continuing saga of the ancient myths of Underworld descent followed by Upperworld rebirth. Joseph Campbell sees "the prime function of mythology as a rite to supply the symbols that carry the human spirit forward, in counteraction to those other constant human fantasies that tend to tie it back" (2008, p. 7). Another view is that some type of emotional and spiritual death—in the language of myth, a "descent to the Underworld" —is a necessary part of psychological maturation and growth.

No one should deny the danger of the descent, but it must be risked. No one need risk it, but it is certain that

Heidi Elowitch (Taylor)

someone will. And let those who go down the sunset way go with open eyes, for it is a sacrifice which daunts even the gods. Yet every descent is followed by an ascent; the vanishing shapes are changed anew, and a truth is validated at the end only if it suffers change and bears new witnesses, new images, in new tongues, like a new wine that is put into new bottles. (Jung, 1952/1967, p. 357)

Transformation through descent is ubiquitous in myth, yet oddly feels like a unique experience to each and every person who falls into the dark depths and arises reinvigorated from the sheer joy of survival, the heroes of their own stories. It is normally not a consciously realized phenomenon that one is living out a universal or collective myth while one is undertaking the journey (or, it might more accurately be said, the journey has taken a hold of the traveler); rather, it is the experience of living through the alchemical fire and emerging as some new thing that enables one to understand at a deep level what it is to be a part of the collective unconscious and to live the myth forward. For those who experience this journey,

it is another variation of the motif of the Hero and the Dragon . . . the Katabasis, the Descent into the Cave. . . . It expresses the psychological mechanism of introversion of the conscious mind into deeper layers of the unconscious psyche. (Jung, as cited in Elder, 2001, para. 1)

The ancient myths have connection to this dissertation topic because they mirror in many ways the journey modern men and women have taken into their own underworlds and emerged to tell the tale. The descent, states Worth, is "a requirement of sovereignty, by which I mean the owning of one's own self and life" (1996, p. 38). The myths of Inanna and Persephone follow.

The Myth of Inanna

The myth of Inanna's descent begins with Inanna, the Queen of Heaven and Earth, having already established a relationship with Enki, the God of Wisdom and Waters. She has been blessed with 14 powers, among them descent into and ascent out of the Underworld. Inanna hears the moaning of her sister Ereshkigal, Queen of the Underworld, and abandons her Upperworld realms of Heaven and Earth to descend into the "great below" (Wolkstein & Kramer, 1983, p. 53). She prepares for the descent by placing her crown upon her head, beads of lapis lazuli around her neck, sparkling stones fastened to her breast (Henderson & Oakes, 1963, p. 102), a gold ring around her wrist, and a royal robe upon her body. She binds a breastplate around her chest and takes a lapis measuring rod and line in her hand. Then she sets out for the *kur*, the netherworld, with her faithful servant Ninshubur. When she arrives at the outer gates of the *kur*, she commands Ninshubur to wait for 3 days, and if she has not returned, to call upon the elder Gods for help (Elder, 2001).

Inanna's descent. When Inanna challenges the gatekeeper to gain entry into the *kur*, he consults with Ereshkigal, telling her that a giant and powerful goddess, arrayed in splendor and with signs of authority, is waiting to enter Her realm. Ereshkigal becomes upset, then tells the gatekeeper to open each gate of the Underworld a mere crack and to remove Inanna's royal garments on her way through (Elder, 2001).

On Inanna's first pass through the gate, he takes her crown. At the second gate, he removes her lapis beads; at the third, off come the sparkling stones; at the fourth, her breastplate; at the fifth, her gold ring; at the sixth, her lapis measuring rod; and at the seventh and final gate, her royal robe. In this naked and helpless fashion, Inanna enters Ereshkigal's throne room. She is instantly surrounded by the Underworld judges, who do not rule in her favor. Ereshkigal then lowers the eye of death upon her sister. She speaks words of wrath against her. She utters the cry of guilt against her. She hits her. Inanna is turned into a corpse, a piece of rotting meat, and thus is hung from "a hook on the wall" (Wolkstein & Kramer, as cited in Elder, 2001, para. 9).

After 3 days have passed, Ninshibur beseeches Enlil, God of Air, on Inanna's behalf, but he flatly refuses to help, for the Underworld is not his domain. Next, Ninshibur goes to Nanna, God of the Moon, who also refuses to help, for he has no jurisdiction over the Underworld. Finally, Ninshibur goes to Enki, God of Wisdom and Water, who had originally blessed Inanna with the *me* of descent into and ascent out of the *kur*. Enki is troubled and grieved by Inanna's plight. From under his fingernails, he takes dirt and creates two genderless creatures, which he provides with the food and water of life to carry to

Inanna. These creatures sneak into the *kur* like flies, slipping through the cracks in the gates. They enter the throne room and find Ereshkigal lying naked and unkempt, moaning, "Oh! Oh! My inside!" Following Enki's instructions, they also moan, "Oh!" Oh! Your inside!" Again she moans, "Ohhhh! Oh! My outside!" The creatures reply, "Ohhh! Oh! Your outside!" She continues to moan out her agony, and they continue to resonate her pains back to her. Finally, she stops moaning, and she blesses the creatures, offering them any gift they wish. They ask for Inanna's corpse, and revive Inanna with the food and water of life. At that point, Inanna arises and ascends to the Upperworld.

Much like human beings who often feel their lot has been preordained by fate in this modern life, Inanna's destiny has been predetermined by Enki. She must experience the pain of the descent to the Underworld precisely because she is the Queen of the Upperworld. Heaven and Earth represent ego, which must take blows in life and learn to recover in order to be truly strong. Life is a progression of cycles, as seen in the changing of the seasons, the passing of nights into days, and other natural phenomena, and mood and affect are not immune from these ups and downs in human nature.

To meet the unconscious requires a turning inward, a depression or lowering of mood and functioning, an intense stillness. An emotionally dead person however, has lost the ability to return to the Upperworld and feels trapped in his or her own personal *kur*. This place is a living death, a place where those who feel trapped wait for the gods to send messengers to save them because they feel they cannot save themselves. Before her descent, Inanna is often called "the pure Inanna" (Henderson & Oakes, as cited in Elder, 2001, "Commentary," para. 2), meaning she is still a child untarnished by the brutality of life, untouched by the darkness of the Underworld. She is not yet whole, not yet complete in her Self, for she has not had a life of full experience. She is still sheltered, safe, protected, and naïve. To be unknowing is to be happy and yet also ignorant and an easy mark. One cannot fully be in the world to any real extent without a full and total knowledge of oneself at a depth level.

Just as Inanna descends, responding to the cries of her distraught sister, the conscious mind lowers itself into that which is weeping, neglected, and wounded; that which remains unhealed in the unconscious mind. The conscious and unconscious must come together and heal one another; the broken person must reintegrate in order to be whole and become a fully functioning Self, a whole which somehow is now something greater than the sum of its parts, because it has seen Heaven and Hell and now walks upon the earth like others. In alchemical terms, the trial-by-fire has made a base rock into the Philosopher's Stone. Nothing good comes easy, and nothing much that comes easy is worth having.

Inanna's descent is not made without a great defense, not approached nakedly. She defends herself with numerous items of clothing and jewelry, representing the conscious mind's or ego's powers to keep the unconscious at bay. One by one, these protective factors are stripped away until there is nothing left with which she may shield herself. It is very interesting to note that

in descending into the depths, the weapons of consciousness become her impediments. The work of descent cannot be done by the well fortified, but only by the vulnerable, by the helpless and disempowered. At the first gate, she must leave her intellectualizing behind. At the second gate, she must quit relying on her cleverness and creativity. At the third gate, her niceness must be surrendered. At the fourth gate, her armor; at the fifth, her ability to do; at the sixth, her critical judgment; and at the final gate, her persona is stripped away from her. She enters the Underworld as naked and helpless as the day she was born. (Elder, 2001, "Commentary," p. 8)

None of the things we commonly rely on to help us in the Upperworld help us in the Underworld: not consciousness, intellectualizing, cleverness, creativity, niceness, armor, the ability to do, critical judgment, nor persona. One enters the Underworld in a naked, vulnerable, and helpless state. It is here that one finds oneself up against one's shadow, judged and crucified, and left to rot slowly away. This is precisely what the depth of depression feels like: an all-encompassing loneliness and lack of escape. Everything one touches decomposes and "turns to shit"; the invasive hopelessness makes one feel powerless to change one's fortune, and one sits in one's own private, hellish misery and waits to rot away.

Inanna's transformation and ascent. In the case of Inanna, her servant Ninshibur represents the remaining part of her consciousness, which still lives while her mood is lowered. Ninshibur is willing to seek help while Inanna lies dying like a corpse. She is willing to take any action, no matter how small, to try to save Inanna. She goes from god to god, none of whom are willing or able to help, until she tries the god who actually created the situation, Enki, the God of Wisdom. Those who are wise learn to accept that darkness is a part of life just as light is, and that no matter how painful, it is a necessary part of growth in order to be a complete Self. It is important to note that Enki's beings do not confront Ereshkigal in the struggle to regain Inanna. They mirror her moans of agony and pain back to her patiently until she voices relief.

> They saw her and heard her pain and did not discount, minimize, question, or blame her. They expressed only compassion and stayed with her. In the presence of acceptance and compassion, Ereshkigal's pain and anger were transformed into gratitude, and as a result, Inanna came back to life. However, as the judges of the underworld informed her, "No one ascends from the Underworld unmarked." (Bolen, 1996, p. 62)

Wisdom knows that depression only begins to heal when hidden pain is recognized, named, and honored; in this way, it is validated and cared for. When Ereshkigal offers the creatures any reward for soothing her agony, they select Inanna, but she is no longer the same, for she now knows both the light and the darkness. One must know what one can bear in order to know oneself truly. "But one must learn to know oneself in order to know who one is. For what comes after the door is, surprisingly enough, a boundless expanse full of unprecedented uncertainty. . . . It is the world of water" (Jung, as cited in Elder, 2001, "Commentary," para. 13).

The meeting with the Underworld forces, be it the rejected items of the ego, the symbolic cries of Ereshkigal the dark sister, the personal unconscious, or the depths of depression, is also a very real and stark meeting with oneself, with all that is one's shadow. It can be completely crippling to confront the shadow self and the horror of the fact that these experiences befall every living creature; there is no living without the confrontation of pain, loss, suffering, grief, bereavement, fear, anxiety, or some other tragic human emotion at some point in time. The more charmed and "perfect" a life someone seems to lead, the more crushing the fall will be when it eventually comes, because the Underworld is a natural part of human existence, the counterpart to the Upperworld, in myth and modernity.

The Myth of Persephone

The myth of Persephone, Greek Goddess of the Underworld, offers a captivating addition to ancient mythic tales of return from the Depth. In this story, on a beautiful, sunny day when the lands are lush with flowers and trees, lovely young Persephone is picking flowers with her friends as her mother, Demeter, watches from nearby and her father, Zeus, watches knowingly from the sky above. Persephone is gathering blooms for her mother when a flower she has never seen before distracts her: a narcissus. As she attempts to reach for it, the earth gives way beneath her feet and her life is forever changed (Strong, 2000).

Persephone's descent. From this blackened hole emerges Hades, God of the Underworld, and he kidnaps Persephone into the very depths of darkness. Persephone ceases to exist in the Upperworld, other than through the pain in her mother's heart. Demeter searches at length for her departed daughter, who is nowhere to be found on earth or in the heavens. Demeter becomes deeply depressed over this tragic loss and is unable to perform her roles as Goddess of Grain and Growth. The decay around her mirrors the decay she feels within (Strong, 2000).

In the Underworld with the dead, Hades attempts to explain himself to Persephone. He proclaims his love, his desire for a wife, and her father's blessing on their union. Persephone yearns for the familiarity and comfort of the Upperworld with her mother's love, daylight, warmth, colors, and the open sky above. She cannot imagine forsaking all she has cherished for a life beneath the ground (Strong, 2000).

Demeter continues her quest in the Upperworld, wandering the barren earth in vain, until she comes to rest by the fountain in Eleusis. She looks and feels older than her years, the pain of great loss having taken its toll on her soul. Demeter continues to press Zeus and the immortals until she discovers what has happened to her daughter. Zeus sends Hermes to retrieve Persephone in an attempt to appease Demeter's growing anger over her daughter's disappearance (Strong, 2000, para. 5).

Persephone's transformation and ascent. By the time Hermes enters the Underworld, Persephone has overcome her initial shock and dismay and is now strong and thriving as the Queen of the Dead. She has taken it as her vocation to help others adjust as they enter the Underworld and have to adapt. She feels torn between her new life and her old one. Hades encourages Persephone to eat from a red pomegranate and explains that he has been selfish and that she must now share herself with the Upperworld as well as the Underworld (Orbis, 2007).

When Demeter's mourning killed all the crops, the mortals had to sustain themselves with what they had left over from prior years. "It was fruit from a previous harvest that sustained Kore, too, while she was in the Underworld" (Orbis, 2007, "Finding Nourishment in the Underworld," para. 1). According to myth, Persephone/Kore inadvertently bound herself to return to the Underworld every year with every pomegranate seed consumed. This can be seen simply as a clever trick of Hades, or more deeply as a conscious choice on the part of Kore to exercise a degree of control in a limiting environment. In this way, she is able actively to nourish herself and thereby digest and integrate her journey into her identity, however small a step it may seem. Kore also uses the seeds to remind her of her mother and her home, as guides to where she will one day return (Orbis, 2007).

Kore has transformed in the Underworld by becoming its Queen. As Hades' bride she became the Lady of the Dead, finding her vocation and destiny as a Goddess presiding over lost souls, thereby coming into her own power, strength, and position of importance. It is at this point that Hermes meets Kore, now Persephone, at the gates to the Underworld to begin the ascent to Demeter, confident that she will return to the Underworld now that it has become her domain. Her identity has broadened; she has re-membered her life in the Upperworld so she can return to visit her mother. Moreover, she has re-membered her *self*, having processed and accepted her painful and difficult experiences without splitting, denying, or dissociating. She owns them as part of herself, thereby allowing her to go down to the Underworld again without fear, since it is now a known place (Orbis, 2007).

Despite the horror of being kidnapped, raped, and made to marry the King of the Underworld, Persephone holds on to the core of who she is. She somehow manages to maintain her sanity and not commit suicide or go unconscious. She retained her clarity and was able to take on a role for herself which not only gave her a sense of strength but also a sense of meaning, assisting others in world she was once forced to navigate alone. Persephone knew better than anyone how terrifying the Underworld could be to new arrivals and was able to guide and assist them in the most appropriate way possible, as a former newcomer herself who not only survived but thrived (Orbis, 2007).

As Persephone returns to the earth to be a daughter again, Demeter brightens with joy, and the flowers begin to bloom once more; yet something does not feel quite the same as it has in the past: Demeter senses that her daughter has changed. She is no longer pure and innocent, as no one can be having been to the Underworld. She has returned from the dead older, wiser, and experienced in worldly ways. Zeus had felt that some type of compromise had to be made; therefore, each spring Persephone returns from the Underworld with flowers to grace her way, representing a return from the deadness of the Depths, bringing with her the possibilities of hope and re-creation. Each fall, when she returns to Hades as Queen of the Underworld, Demeter feels sorrow and the earth turns cold while she awaits Persephone's return. For Persephone, however, there is no longer despair; she has made peace with the time she spends as Underworld guide to those who have lost their direction in the next phase of life (Strong, 2000).

Death as a Process of Transformation

Heidi Elowitch (Taylor)

As Bonnano and Kaltman (1999) state, "the death of a loved one is a ubiquitous human experience; most people at some point in their lives, must confront the inevitable, and in many cases enduring, pain of interpersonal loss" (p. 125). Universally, the death process has been a struggle, both literally and figuratively. According to Bolen,

> to enter into a depth psychological process is to knock at a gate to the   Underworld. Nightmares; repetitious dreams; unbidden thoughts, images, and impulses; pervasive anxiety; depression; inability to know what one really feels; deep unhappiness are some of the reasons for making a descent, through which it may be possible to be a witness, to feel, know, remember, and mourn what lies below. (1996, p. 55)

The soul interprets death not as the opposite of life, but as the opposite of birth. In mythic terms, the Underworld, considered the realm of the dead, is a place of liminality and transformation, a temporary return to primordial chaos prior to rebirth into a new state of being. As in all initiations, the completion of the transformation requires the intercession of a greater community of beings who can facilitate the burial of the old form. Proper burial is a major theme in Greek myth, as seen in *The Iliad* and *The Odyssey* where main characters visit the Underworld to conduct burial rights or to grieve at funerals. Major tragic dramas often focus on the theme of burial, or burial denied, as well. Current psychology refers to this as "closure," but there is no agreement about the meaning of this term.

Tales of Awakening

The myths reflect the belief that death is a process, not a single event; the dead require the focused acts of the living in order to complete their transition to another world. The living need this process also, because souls who wander in the liminal space in between worlds eventually cause suffering for the living. Unburied dead in particular were considered to haunt relatives. These souls were seen as "stuck," unable to complete the end of life's processes and be welcomed home by their ancestors. They were imagined to exist somewhere between worlds, like certain mentally ill persons (Spector, 2005).

In indigenous funeral customs, the proper transition to death requires an extensive involvement of the living. A number of rites and rituals must take place in order for closure to occur. Although on the surface this appears to be only an effort to help the deceased person transition smoothly to the next phase and complete his or her journey with no hindrance, it is also very much a ritual that allows the mourners to complete their grieving and move on into healing. The current standard of swift funeral rituals in modern society creates the opposite of closure and institutes a type of denial. "When those in mourning have not given sufficient time and emotional attention to the grief process, the wounds close too soon and remain infected. It is the inability to achieve emotional closure that haunts the American soul" (Spector, 2005, online).

Illness as Soul Sickness in the Underworld

Jean Shinoda Bolen describes crossing the transitory state from health to illness as a time of "entering the realm of the soul" (1996, p. 14). This is a time when

> we lose an innocence, we know vulnerability, we are no longer who we were before this event, and we will never be the same. We are in uncharted terrain, and there is no turning back. Illness is a profound soul event, and yet this is virtually ignored and unaddressed. (p. 14)

Illness may encompass much more than just physical ailments and disease. To look at the picture broadly, illness can include physical illness, mental illness such as depression, emotional despair, soul sickness, and spiritual sickness as well as heartbreak, grief, loss, and still more nebulous forms of personal and individual pain and suffering. This life at the edge, "in the border realm between life and death" (p. 15) is what Bolen describes as being lived in "a *liminal* time and place" (p. 15). She notes that *liminal* comes from the Latin word for *threshold*, indicating participation in something that will alter one and shift how others relate to one, similar to being initiated into new knowledge or experiencing new cultural rites of passage. In the case of a liminal experience, the "mystical, spiritual, or psychic awareness of what is happening determines its significance as a soul experience" (p. 15).

Liminal experiences make one keenly aware of how fleeting and delicate life is. They make one take a hard look at one's priorities and rearrange them if they are not in good order.

One may see where one has been shallow or blind or fooling oneself and decide to come clean. One may suddenly see who and what truly does and does not matter and be willing to let certain things go in order to instill more energy into the crucial ones. Spiritual and religious beliefs are changed, shaped, created, and abandoned as one goes through this journey. One becomes a new person after such trials, for having gone through the alchemical process, no one can remain base metal even if one has not quite become the philosopher's stone. One starts to think about what one has left undone, all the unfinished business, all the things one wants to accomplish or learn before one dies, and one begins to feel the pressure of time. One may ask, who or what do I want to reconnect with from the past? Who or what is needlessly draining my time, effort, and energy that I would like to cut loose? One may start to think more deeply about one's dreams and odd synchronicities and what messages they offer.

Bolen (1996) rightly points out that when one is in the throes of such a state of affairs, one is in a moment of baring one's soul, naked and vulnerable, fragile, and easily hurt by criticism or a lack of understanding. This is especially tricky because soul-baring moments are so real and raw that they can be quite frightening and overwhelming to the uninitiated. The first and often the only impulse is to soothe, quiet, suppress, cover up, stifle, and silence that which is unfamiliar and seems beyond one's ability to cope with. It is like coming up against a fire-breathing

Heidi Elowitch (Taylor)

dragon, flying into a panic and trying to make it stop; but breathing fire is simply the nature of the creature, and it cannot and should not be changed. Trying to do so would be where the difficulties ensue, for both the dragon and its assailant or even its self-titled rescuer. Bolen writes:

> The impulse of others is to hurriedly cover up our words with a thin layer of reassurance—to which we respond by withdrawing. Revealing matters of the soul makes those who dwell in shallower waters uncomfortable. Soul-searching questions are those that people who are addicted to work or to alcohol or to superficial activities are warding off by their addictions. They do not want to be exposed to their own deep questions, as voiced by us. (p. 18)

According to Bolen (1996), "spiritual or psychological resurrection" (p. 55) results in one being significantly transformed. Death is a major, recurring metaphor in the language of the soul, encompassing death of the old personality in order to make way for the rebirth, resurrection, or transformation of the new personality. At first there may be numbness, then terror, when one realizes one's old self and old life are dead. The death of the illusion that one had control over these things is the hardest part to accept. If one meets one's soul successfully along the underworld journey, new discoveries about who and what one is and can be are slowly made and celebrated as a new beginning. Mourning of the ending is the beginning of healing. So begins a new life and a new search for meaning arising from unwanted and unchosen circumstances. The will to persevere depends upon finding a meaning in it all. Bolen muses:

> When life is lived at the edge—in the border realm between life and death—it is a *liminal* time and place. *Liminal* comes from the Latin word for "threshold." It is not an everyday word; it is one whose meaning I want to evoke out of the remembered experience of the reader and the collective memory of the human race, which we all have access to. Whenever we participate in something that will change us, and change how others relate to us—as when we marry, are inducted into the armed forces or ordained, become a doctor, or survive an ordeal—that experience is a liminal one. (p. 15)

The passage through a liminal time and place may evoke feelings of fear, despair, helplessness, paralysis, numbness, anxiety, chaos, and vulnerability as one navigates uncharted territory. Out of this richly fertile soil emerges the possibility for growth, transformation, the ability to love without fear, and enlightenment. The floodgates of the block of limitations have been released, allowing a deeper engagement with life.

The Arc of Eros

The chaos that ensues in one's "ordinary life" when traumatic experiences like illness strike open one to the liminal experience Bolen (1996) describes. Goodchild (2001) notes accurately that "in moments of chaotic breakdown—of either an individual or a collective nature, when our familiar and cherished positions become unraveled—or alternatively, in those moments of deep loving, we are perhaps most open to such experiences" (p. xx). She continues:

> Love, then, is difficult and demanding, perhaps the most difficult accomplishment of all. But the mythic figure of Eros is not an easy figure. He spans an arc from the sublime to the disastrous, from bliss to despair, which intuitively makes sense if we reflect even momentarily on our experiences with love and the messes it can create in our lives. (p. xxx)

In her discussion of the influence of Eros, Goodchild draws on ancient myths that unite Eros and Chaos. Exploring the world of depression through the imaginal realm begins with the Greek myth of Chaos, the first God, the "formless void of darkness out of which all things possible arose" (Kiehl, 2005, "The Imaginal Realm of Depression," para. 1). It then follows that Eros, "fairest among the deathless Gods" (Hesiod, as cited in "The Imaginal Realm of Depression," para. 1) brings a clarity and depth to the understanding of the phenomenology of depression. Whereas one's ability to love is born out of one's soul being in a state of chaos, this mirrors the concept in poetic reverie of light entering the soul's darkness. In depression one relates to an interior relationship with the Gods of Chaos; when emerging from depression one shifts to the realm of exterior relationships with the Gods of Eros.

Kiehl (2005) sees this process of searching for light in the darkness as making us more human by keeping us in contact with parts of ourselves that we otherwise would overlook or ignore. Our lack of relating to those parts of self creates a sense of loneliness and estrangement from our core. If one makes peace with the void, one not only knows oneself and life's mysteries more fully, but begins to yearn for relationship outside the void:

> Eventually, we begin a desire to move towards outer relationship, to carry back the message that we are not alone. We reach out and perceive the world, experience the world as a lived experience. Thus giving birth to the coniunctio, the uniting of I and Thou. We emerge out of the darkness, experiencing a joining with the world. Beauty facilitates this birthing process. Beauty awakens our desire to relate, beauty in the feminine, beauty in the Word. Awakening us to reverie in life, reverie to breath [sic] life back into our souls. Living in reverie means celebrating beauty in all forms. Opening awareness to seeing, sensing, hearing, feeling the beauty in the world, this is the concretization of relation, making Eros present in our lives. Bringing soul to Matter is the immanent coniunctio. And with this return, this carrying back of our soul into body, we experience the reverie of life. ("The Imaginal Realm of Depression," para. 8)

Considering the myths discussed in this review, both center around the joy and pathos of love. Inanna lowers herself out of love and compassion for Ereshkigal and yet is gravely betrayed, and Ereshkigal is healed by the genderless little beings sent to console her out of unconditional love and therein finds her own compassion. Persephone is cruelly abducted by Hades and yet grows to love him, Hades learns to become less selfish out of love for Persephone and empathy for her agonized mother Demeter, and Demeter grows spiritually to find joy with Persephone by her side only part of the time.

Goodchild (2001) examines other aspects of the "suffering shadows of love, particularly the themes of abandonment and abandoning, through the image of the Orphan" (p. xxx). She muses on how "suffering invites us to surrender into the unknown, and to surrender our attachments to old structures that no longer serve the soul" (p. xxx). stating, "In such a fall or wounding we can also find our true vocation, a call that connects us with our vertical fate or destiny" (p. xxxi). It is interesting to note that in times of great loss, rather than cling desperately to anything around in the hope of finding comfort or staying afloat, there is often an otherworldly strength or a simple grace in being able to let go and release that which is no longer pertinent or nourishing to one's soul. It is as if being rendered broken and alone makes it impossible to consider anything a loss instead of a gain. There is a new sense of freedom and release from the shackles that bound one to old burdens and commitments that drained one's time, energy, and effort. The soul suddenly realizes that it cannot soar if it is being held down by leaden weights, and it cannot be free to embrace something new if it is still clinging to the shattered shards of the past.

Goodchild (2001) emotes:

Tales of Awakening

To love and be loved is arguably the only thing that most of us would rather not exit this life without knowing. In my experience as a therapist, most people come into therapy in search of love, no matter what the presenting problem. Fame, fortune, and even mediocrity may come and go, but love participates in the substance of the universe itself, and is eternal. Love ceases not. Once you have loved and been loved, it can never be taken away; not even at death, such is the imprint in the cells of our souls. Love is that eternal landscape that takes us beyond life, beyond death, even beyond rebirth. (p. 9)

This is the love that those in the Upperworld carry for those in the Underworld while they are below. It is the love felt for one's soul-mates and loved ones after they have passed and that one feels they still carry for us. It is even the sense of love one had for one's body before it became ill or injured and the sense of love one learns to develop for one's body as it has become. There are many kinds of love, but once a person has known love, he or she cannot un-know it. It remains with one forever in one form or another.

In her chapter, "The Mysteries and Shadows of Love," Goodchild (2001) cites powerful quotes as reminders that the soul is made terribly vulnerable to the Underworld journey by the woundings of love: "In a love relation, as Jung once put it, you risk everything" (von Franz, as cited in Goodchild, 2001, p. 21); "Yet to sing love, love must first shatter us" (H. D., as cited in Goodchild, p. 21). Some type of harrowing experience causes one to fall into the abyss: a tragic loss, of love, of life, of health, of safety, of personal or mental integrity, and so on. Finding one's way back to the Upperworld is a long, risky, painful, scary, uncertain journey. The details of the stories indicate how different heroines and survivors make the transition from place to place. The prompting, stimulus or stimuli, journey, path, or outcome are not the same for everyone who has the experience. From Inanna's bizarre rebirth to Persephone's equally odd living compromise, who knows what other means of survival and return modern-day individuals have manifested or experienced in order to survive the yawning darkness. Goodchild (2001) points out a painful truism:

> Seeking the elixir of life is always dangerous because what always comes up in the search are duality, dissociation, repression, and the face of one's own dark twin. We have to confront the truth that destruction is the other side of creation; they belong inexorably together. Every incremental step in consciousness ruthlessly involves both forces. Perhaps another way to imagine this story is that life sought consciously always brings the reality and knowledge of death, loss, and dismemberment. Jung speaks of this darkness as containing the seeds of much gold, since the recovery of the wholeness that we lose in becoming conscious is achieved by the willingness to tread through the minefields of our experience and live such experience fully. (p. 40)

Chodron (1997) describes the experience of things falling apart as a cloaked opportunity to advance on a karmic developmental level:

What we're talking about is getting to know fear, becoming familiar with fear, looking it right in the eye—not as a way to solve problems, but as a complete undoing of old ways of seeing, hearing, smelling, tasting, and thinking. The truth is that when we really begin to do this, we're going to be continually humbled. (p. 3)

She views times of chaos and stress as periods of transition, which can remind one to relax and go with the flow if one can accept the inevitable fear and commit to the voyage. To hear that "chaos should be regarded as extremely good news" (p. xi) is more than enough to make the hairs on the back of one's neck stand up. This paradigm shift involves an entirely new way of viewing change and upheaval. It can only be embraced once one has had the experience of surviving such a state of affairs and lived to tell the tale. Such a feat creates a state of faith, a belief in something greater than oneself. It allows one to believe that one is exactly where one is supposed to be, experiencing exactly what one is supposed to be experiencing, exactly when one is supposed to be experiencing it, even if one does not know why or it does not make sense at the time.

The trick is to keep exploring and not bail out, even when we find out that something is not as we thought. That's what we're going to discover again and again and again. Emptiness . . . mindfulness . . . fear . . . compassion . . . love. . . Buddha nature . . . courage. These are words that point to what life really is when we let things fall apart and let ourselves be nailed to the present moment. (p. 5)

A state of grace is what allows one to believe there is a lesson to be learned in all happenings, good or bad. Such a developmental leap creates a more spiritual life filled with a greater sense of peace and security. One is no longer afraid to let go of the rope because one knows there will be a net there to catch one's fall.

Hillman makes the point that that "by refusing chaos, we are in danger of losing eros, too. . . . [Eros] renews itself in affective attacks, jealousies, fulminations, and turmoils. It thrives close to the dragon" (as cited in Goodchild, 2001, p. 29). Eros is a sticky, tricky character, full of zest and zeal and drama. There is nothing mild-mannered about it. There is no great love without great chaos, and no great chaos that leaves love unharmed. Intense feeling opens one up to the possibility of severe loss, and yet, paradoxically, major loss can lead one down into the realm of the soul and allow for the discovery of new strengths, interests, coping abilities, and survival skills, culminating in the return of a different, often stronger, person from the one whose life is untouched by eros and chaos. By stating that Eros "thrives close to the dragon," Hillman implies that eros is felt the strongest when one is in danger of some sort—in danger of losing the source of one's eros, of losing oneself in eros, of becoming separated from the object of one's eros, or of taking the treacherous journey hoping to find eros in an eros-less life. The dragon is no small competitor, and one must become a brave and courageous warrior to contend with the dragon or it is a lost cause.

In Western culture, thinking has continuously shifted chaos into the mental position of "Other," as something different and not a part of being human (Goodchild, 2001). Chaos is seen as something having to do particularly with the female experience and has been "mostly marginalized as feminine, especially in its cyclical, sensual, erotic, dark, rhythmic, and transformational dimensions" (p. 34). This is in rather sharp contrast to the "patriarchal ego's attachment to reasonable, linear, unchanging ideals that delude us into thinking that we are protected from the overpowering and predictable—otherwise known as Life" (p. 34).

Many people are mesmerized by the grand delusion that they live far from the dragon, until it opens its mouth and breathes fire on them, leaving them in flames, charred, or it opens its big mouth and devours them alive. The dragon is always close at hand; sometimes it may be deep within its lair or may be disguised as a bright and intriguing character rather than a dangerous monster. In martial arts lore, the dragon is the only mythical animal upon which forms are based, and it is known for being the only creature adept at fighting on all three planes: on land, in the sea, and in the sky (United Studios of Self Defense, 1990). Viewed another way, the dragon exists everywhere and is not hindered in its ability to travel through barriers that stump lesser beasts.

Fear of the Dragon

Heidi Elowitch (Taylor)

People often hesitate in facing life's challenges and opportunities for growth for fear of this "dragon." Chodron (1997) states that "fear is a natural reaction to moving closer to the truth" (p. 1). In other words, any journey that takes one closer to a spiritual awakening or a universal lesson or experience is likely to be accompanied by a degree of fear and apprehension. On a depth level, even journeys which would normally be regarded as positive and joyous, such as marriage or having a child, should rightfully be approached with a well-deserved degree of awe and trepidation. They too contain within them unknown truths and are therefore to be regarded with a bit of fear. One can only imagine the amount of terror contained in the truths approached through deaths of loved ones, divorces, sickness, rape, or some such other casualty. Although one will always benefit from moving closer to the truth, and therefore closer to the light, the fear one has to confront in doing so is not to be taken lightly. Chodron believes that people should consider themselves lucky to confront fear because it teaches them courage (p. 5).

Chodron (1997) raises the concept of not "concretizing" (p. 6), of not allowing fear and pain to make one become rigid and immobile. Part of the challenge of great suffering is learning how to flex, to develop new skills and depths of coping one never had before and never realized as a possibility. This changes both the personal and the professional approach to dealing with trauma. It becomes much less frightening, less intimidating, less of an enemy to be overcome.

Martin (1996) explored the reactions of women diagnosed with breast cancer. She discovered that although the women she interviewed were very different from each other, they all reacted to their cancer diagnosis by undergoing transformation. They experienced profound attitudinal changes toward life as a direct result of the pain of confronting illness and all of its ramifications. There is no way to confront a chronic or terminal illness or the death of a loved one and not have some type of reaction to it. In the best of cases, the initial shock and grief can give way to a lesson that can be learned in few other ways.

Confronting illness helps one to see what is truly important, it makes clear that time is finite and one must accomplish things now if one is going to do them at all. Time is not as unlimited as one might have allowed oneself to think in one's oblivious pre-illness state. Illness is a wake-up call that helps one to get a sharper focus and a clearer perspective on what is truly important in one's life that is simply not possible to get within an "ordinary" existence free from upheaval.

When pain hits, life can fragment and scatter in different directions. One may experience disintegration, disconnection, decompensation, and metaphorical dismemberment. When the world as one knows it blows apart, it is difficult if not impossible to re-member oneself, to put back together the pieces that have separated, gotten lost, warped, remain unaccounted for, and are sometimes unidentifiable. It may seem impossible or make no sense to try to put a person back together out of the parts left. Woodman (2000) talks about dismembering in her book, *Bone: Dying into Life*, documenting her journey through diagnosis, treatment, and triumph over cancer. She states that she lost her "sense of purpose" (p. 29). "I was dis-membered," she wrote, "lost center. Now I am re-membering, gathering together the prodigal parts of myself and welcoming them home" (p. 29).

The Trickster and Chaos

The Trickster is an archetypal figure infamous as the universal deliverer of psychological as well as physical, mental, emotional, spiritual, and environmental chaos (D. Sharpe, personal communication, 2002). One knows one has encountered Trickster when one feels in the presence of something that is outside the realm of one's normal range of experience. The defining commonality of a trickster-based experience is the sensation of having no framework within which to interpret the experience, no guidelines to make sense of what is happening (D. Sharpe, personal communication, 2002). Under the influence of the trickster, there is a glaring absence of the usual rules or patterns that govern one's life; one is at a loss to know how to handle matters effectively. The more one attempts to apply old methods, the more frustrated and befuddled one becomes. Encountering the Underworld or the emotionally dead zone is very much an experience dominated by the trickster, so much so that one may not even know one is in a terribly altered state until one comes out of it (Luckert, as cited in Rutsky, 1998, p. xiii).

When one has encountered the trickster, one's old ways of coping with life are useless, and one is forced to make exponential leaps in personal growth, to branch out in new and different ways. One most often is forced to grow through pain when in the presence of the trickster. Whether by forcing one to come face to face with illness, addiction, gender issues, bereavement, or any other number of possibilities, the trickster throws a wrench into one's normal range of being and literally stretches or breaks open the self and forces it to adapt to new stimuli formerly beyond its grasp. Although it is dreadful while it is occurring, confrontation with the trickster oddly leaves one stronger and more flexible and adept at coping than one was before being graced with its presence. "Trickster the culture hero is always present; his seemingly asocial actions continue to keep our world lively and give it the flexibility to endure" (Hyde, 1998, p. 9).

The most wrenching and overwhelming experiences in one's life are, paradoxically, the times with the potential for the greatest growth, if one survives them. It takes an array of qualities to survive a battle with the trickster. Wits, cunning, intelligence, humor, resiliency, flexibility, compassion, and fortitude are among the most helpful. One must be able to match wills with the trickster, to outsmart him or her, to laugh off or laugh through some of the ploys, to bend and stretch as never before, to know when to lay low and when to come out guns a-blazing, to be able to bounce back and keep trying when one has not quite succeeded, yet be gentle and forgiving with oneself and others, and to be strong and determined not to give up in the face of sometimes frightening odds.

It can help to have sympathy and empathy for the trickster itself; rather than thinking of it as an enemy, try imagining it simply as what it is. Trickster energy may not deliberately try to bring one to ruin, it simply does what it does because that is its function. "The Devil is an agent of evil, but trickster is *a*moral, not *im*moral. He embodies and enacts that large portion of our experience where good and evil are hopelessly intertwined" (Hyde, 1998, p. 10).

It can be useful to try to work with trickster energy rather than against it. This way, one can harness some of the trickster's energy and put it to positive use in treacherous circumstances. One trick is to play dead, as if having given up the fight. The trickster thinks, "Ah-ha! I can rest a bit!" Then one can try something new and unusual that the trickster was not expecting. Another trick is to pretend to have joined the trickster's fight and to have the same goal. The trickster will think, "I don't need to work as hard if both of us are working together!" Once the trickster slows down, one might be able to overtake him or her. Another option is to stop working and wait for the trickster to become fatigued. This is a ripe time to make one's move. It takes patience, cleverness, and persistence to contend with the trickster energy once it has entered one's life. One thing is for sure, though; if one does not attempt to harness trickster energy, the trickster will easily succeed:

> Trickster is at one and the same time creator and destroyer, giver and negator, he who dupes others and is always duped himself. . . . He knows neither good nor evil yet he is responsible for both. He possesses no values, moral or social . . . yet through his actions all values come into being. (Hyde, 1998, p. 10)

It is best to have faith in the unfolding of the process; there is a reason it is happening, even if one does not know that reason yet or may never understand the reason. If one believes that there is a reason for everything that happens and that everything happens for a reason, then there are no accidents. It is possible that everyone is in the right place at the right time, exactly where they need to be to learn whatever lesson they have come into the world to learn. Having faith in the necessity of the event, however awful or disturbing, makes it more bearable. Surrendering rather than fighting against it frees up resources that can help repair and heal. People who meet the trickster and deal with it become the heroes of their own journeys. It is at this crux that the trickster becomes the transformer, the impetus for emerging from the blackness and into the light. "In understanding the trickster better, we better understand ourselves and the perhaps subconscious aspects of ourselves that respond to the trickster's unsettling and transformative behavior" (Lock, 2002, para. 1).

In certain cases, the trickster can be seen as the impetus causing people to fight their own personal demons. Native Americans assign the role of trickster to the Coyote and call alcoholism, drug addiction, and other illnesses "coyote sickness" (Rutzky, 1998, p. xiii). The sickness is a combination of internal demons and external influences and requires the performance of a cleansing and healing ritual by a shaman or medicine man to help the sufferers make reparations for their offenses, regain their power, and become centered once more. The Navaho believe that sickness comes from activities that distort social relationships, break taboos, and fulfill self-indulgence. Illness arises from contact with a "substance outside the natural order of harmony and beauty" (Rutzky, 1998, p. xiii).

Rutzky (1998) elucidates some fascinating parallels between the trickster's activities and the path of addicts in recovery:

> Still using, newly sober, or years into recovery . . . one may notice characteristics of this trickster in alcoholics and addicts: slipping into your office under the cover of darkness (his denial, your ignorance, or lack in experience), wearing the skin of another animal (the presenting problem may be depression, anxiety, marital, work, or health problems), stealing something (your good will, your good judgment, your compassion, your patience), and like many people in crisis, creating havoc in your professional life (by not following through with agreements, canceling appointments, or failing to maintain sobriety), and blaming

it on someone else (work, stress, or a lack of understanding in others). (p. 2)

Anyone who has dealt with addiction in one form or another—be it one's own, that of a friend or loved one, or a patient's or client's—is sure to recognize the bright and shiny hallmarks of the trickster in action. The trickster is so potent, so quick to take action, so devious, underhanded, duplicitous, deceitful, conniving, and gluttonous in addiction that it may well be the most insurmountable area in which to confront him or her. For most addicts, the trickster tells them they do not have a chance to succeed or that they do not even want to, so why bother trying?

The trickster is famous for lying, cheating, and stealing in an effort to get what he or she wants; so is an addict in the grip of addiction. The urge to use at all costs makes addicts and alcoholics sacrifice their jobs, careers, families, love lives, reputations, self-esteem, and health in order to use or drink and satisfy the trickster. Rutzky (1998) notes another unpleasant similarity between Coyote as trickster and practicing alcoholics and addicts: they are "virtually incapable of reflecting on the pain they cause themselves and others because they have a difficult time admitting their own flaws and failings" (p. 2). The alcoholic or addict may have problems with this due to being intoxicated, hung-over, detoxing, withdrawing, having blackout-induced memory loss, brain damage, intentional hiding and covering up to keep the use a secret from family, and preventing problems leading to arrest or prosecution for use. Rutzky states that "in order to maintain his distorted sense of reality, Coyote blames others for his problems and holds tight to his blindness. For the alcoholic and addict, this means defending against the growing tide of substance-related problems by embracing denial" (p. 2).

A Navaho story, "Coyote and His Reflection," captures this concept with crystal clarity (Rutzky, 1998). Coyote goes to the water to take a drink, but his own reflection frightens him so that he thinks he is seeing a monster. He runs away and watches the lake. Other animals drink without showing fear, but every time Coyote tries to drink, he again sees the hideous monster. Finally, a frog speaks to Coyote. Coyote is rude and mean and tells Frog he is ugly. Frog tells Coyote to just keep his eyes closed if he does not like what he sees. So Coyote closes his eyes. "With his eyes closed he saw nothing and so nothing frightened him. Nothing tried to catch him. And nothing scared him" (p. 3). This is the mechanism by which those in the grip of addiction go through their lives, refusing to see the damage they are doing to themselves and others, including society. When one is owned, so to speak, by a substance, it is too painful to live in the here and now of day-to-day reality. It is only tolerable to get through the pain of losing oneself and everything one cares about by checking-out, delusion, and refusal to see what is right before one's eyes. This delusion and refusal is contagious: it transmits to those around the addict or alcoholic who collude in the charade, believing the excuses, lies, and flimsy explanations, while filled with gnawing doubts and anguish about what is really going on.

This is the disease of codependency so common in friends and family of addicts and alcoholics, but which is also prevalent in professional mental health practitioners in the field. Such is the nature of trickster that he or she can pull the wool over their eyes. Rutzky (1998) relates an amusing and astute quote relating to Jung's archetypal Trickster as it appears in psychotherapy:

> Coyote's greatest delusion, that he knows everything, is frequently my own delusion as well... And though I know with great certainty that Coyote will never be destroyed, I can, at least, recognize his familiar shape, smell, and howl when he comes into my office, sniffs the furniture, and plops down beside me, smiling. (p. 9)

How often do we as family members, partners, friends, clinicians, forget that we do not know everything? How often do we forget that Coyote will never be eradicated? Most importantly, how often do we let our guard down, become falsely secure, and fail to recognize Coyote's familiar shape and smell when he or she comes and sits down next to us, smiling? How often do we not want to see Coyote, or worse yet, see him or her but convince ourselves we must be mistaken because to admit one sees Coyote is to open up a panorama of difficulties we would prefer to avoid? As Rutzky (1998) says, working with alcoholics and addicts is about pointing to the water, looking in together, and not drinking or using. It is about facing the pain of life stone-cold sober. It is about helping addicts and alcoholics find another way to confront the monster without telling them to close their eyes. (p. 4)

One of the most basic ways of accomplishing this task is through the use of 12-step programs, which parallel the methods and goals of native shamanic rituals in many ways. The steps encourage participants to examine behavior, make amends for wrongs to self and others, reconnect with the self and the Holy, and become more spiritual and connected to the earth and the community. Psychotherapy and the building of a holding space or safe container for processing loaded affects and achieving ultimate wholeness is another basic building block in treatment. The aim is to increase the capacity for self-awareness, insight, and consciousness at a pace smooth enough to avoid flooding or the promotion of a relapse but not so slow as to stagnate.

Flores (1997) relates:

In treating addicted patients . . . confrontation is essential at the beginning of treatment. The focus should not be on the alcoholics' or addicts' unconscious assumptions; rather, one must constantly point out to them the external aspects of their behavior. The purpose of treatment during the initial stages of recovery is to do for the alcoholics or addicts what they are unable to do for themselves. Because their denial is so strong and their pathological defenses so rigid, they require a strong, caring relationship with a group leader who will serve as a container for their anger and anxiety while pointing out, in a nonpunitive manner, the destructive patterns of their behavior. Learning to successfully confront requires (1) timing, (2) the capacity to successfully form an alliance, and (3) empathy. If these skills are not adequately developed, group members will respond defensively, withdraw emotionally, attack the group and its members because of their own fears, or drop out of treatment. (p. 585)

It takes courage to grapple with an opponent as tricky and filled with guile as the Coyote. Patients, clients, family, friends, partners, and practitioners must not give up hope or allow themselves to become discouraged and admit defeat at the hands of the trickster; rather, they must learn how to twist and turn with the hands of fate so that they become stronger, more competent, and more capable at meeting Coyote not just on Coyote's terms but also their own. They can grow from these experiences with the trickster into more fully resonant and functional human beings with a greater range of capabilities and a richer fund of knowledge and skills. The trickster has a way of appearing in each person's life, at one point or another, as one of those archetypal, universal experiences of growth and enlightenment. These occasions are both oddly painful and wryly funny: just when one thinks one has learned the lesson, another one is sure to hit.

Through his negotiation with and disruption of rules and boundaries, the trickster by implication enlarges the sphere of human possibility, or at least the sphere that his human listeners can through identification with the trickster imagine to be possible for themselves. (Lock, 2002, para. 5)

Heidi Elowitch (Taylor)

Choosing Life Through Death

Confronting the Trickster element when chaos enters one's life takes courage. In his book, *Suicide and the Soul*, Hillman (1997) states, "Some choose life because they are afraid of death and others choose death because they are afraid of life. We cannot justly assess courage or cowardice from the outside" (p. 64). Many addicts seem to choose a slow form of death because it is so difficult, painful, and frightening to face life. From the outside this may seem like escapism and avoidance of the problem or a lack of confronting the issue, but it may be the most direct way of dealing with a problem that some depressed individuals have available to them when they see no other solutions open. By contrast, many individuals in deep depression cling to life by threads, only because the specter of death is more terrifying than the trauma of living in the Underworld, or a living death. It is impossible to judge which is braver or more cowardly, for each attitude can be seen in either light depending on the viewer and the vantage point at a given time in space.

Hillman (1997) states that *"death appears in order to make way for transformation"* (p. 67). It is not possible for new blossoms to appear on a plant while the dead blooms are in their way. A tree cannot bear new fruit if its limbs are weighed down with rotting remains from last season's harvest. People tend their gardens, cut them back, and pull weeds; they trim their hair and nails; and they bury their dead to make room for new lives. This is the literal manifestation of something that is equally true metaphorically. Change occurs in letting go of old ideas, outdated prejudices, invalid beliefs, and unproven hypotheses and by entertaining newer theories, fresh ideas, and bright new paradigms that turn that former worldview upside down. One's outlook or perspectives and one's thoughts, feelings, and beliefs about things change many times over a lifetime. Only death allows new life. One ending can become another beginning.

Hillman makes the crucially important point that "analysis is a prolonged 'nervous breakdown'" (1997, p. 68) and that "*analysis means dying*" (p. 68). He further states that "resistance can not be taken superficially. . . . It is illusory to hope that growth is but an additive process requiring neither death nor sacrifice" (p. 68). One may have to "die" many times, in many ways, in order truly to live. As Hillman states, "an analyst may encourage his patient to experience these events, to welcome them, even to treasure them—for some get better by getting worse" (p. 159). With great eloquence, Hillman summarizes the experience of transformation through tragedy: "Dipped into oblivion by this experience, one emerges without knowing precisely what has happened; one only knows that one has been changed" (p. 179).

The tragedy one suffers may be due to grief over the illness or death of a loved one. Boss and Couden (2002) studied ambiguous loss from chronic physical illness as it affects individuals, couples, and families. Their case study demonstrates that

> lack of clarity about prognosis, daily physical condition, and fluctuating capabilities create relationship confusion, preoccupation with the illness, or avoidance of the ill individual. Immobilization, depression, and relationship collapse may occur in response to features of chronic illness over which there is no control. (p. 1351)

Adams (1995) shares the reactions of survivors of the suicide of a loved one, including her own images, dreams, and ideations. She takes a heuristic approach to the exploration of the complex grief process of death via suicide, and how it changes those left behind (p. 22). Dream journal entries and researcher commentaries during the process were all incorporated into her dissertation work. Survivors stated that their therapeutic relationships were important but that the most crucial need was for their individual grieving to be respected. Jungian depth psychology emphasizing archetypes was used to integrate the suicide for these participant-survivors.

Important discoveries regarding the treatment of grief in today's culture were made by Fidel-Rice (2002), who says that American society neither acknowledges nor respects the process of grief-work and thereby leaves the bereaved adrift and frozen (p. 15). The level of denial regarding death and dying has prevented a depth approach from being taken in treating survivors of loss (p. 3). Fidel-Rice describes grief recovery as a process that can be aided by the inclusion of an alchemical consciousness opening people to new levels of experience (p. 31). In her work, an alchemical approach to grief-work proved effective for psychological intervention, personal transformation, and collective healing (p. 172).

The Need for Research on the Topic in Clinical Psychology

This dissertation is directed toward the needs of people going through forms of loss and grief, be it loss of a relationship, loss of health, separation through death, suffering through mental illness, or any of the other myriad miseries of pain, grief, tragedy, and isolation in the human condition. Depression is often an underlying symptom of the preceding common situations in life. This study is intended to show that for many people, even in the darkest hour of sliding into that tunnel of despair and lying stagnant in the well, when it seems that one is a permanent dweller in the Underworld, an eventual dawning of a new day occurs above ground. The period of rebirth and re-emergence is different for everyone, but it does happen.

The understanding of how this transformative shift comes about offers a view people can relate to when they feel like a stranger in a strange land, misunderstood or rejected by the world around them, even those they would have expected to support them above all. The documentation of the experiences of others

Heidi Elowitch (Taylor)

who have survived the descent into the Underworld and ascended with a new sense of life might provide an element of hope to hold onto for those who are in a bleak and empty space, feeling there is nothing to live for. It can provide the essence of being understood (B. Grote, personal communication, March 12, 2004.), an element which alone can be lifesaving when one feels disconnected, alone in a sea of chaos and despair.

In her praise for Jean Shinoda Bolen's *Close to the Bone: Life-Threatening Illness and the Search for Meaning*, Isabel Allende says:

> This is the book I needed when my daughter was sick. It would have helped me through it, like a map of the underworld. Myths, stories, prayer, touching, visualization, rituals, and especially love are some of the tools and wisdom that this extraordinary book gives us. (as cited in Bolen, 1996, frontispiece)

I have endeavored to create a research-oriented dissertation that will meet this ideal. It is intended to inform therapists and, in its eventual form as a book, to help a modern-day Inanna or Persephone (and those that care for them), suddenly thrust into the living death of the Underworld, understand her experience and have faith that there will be a return to a life in the Upperworld again.

It is my deepest wish that this project might contribute a new slant on a pressing issue, offer guidance to practitioners and students, and most of all, give hope to those who suffer at the cold

Tales of Awakening

and numbing hands of depression and grief. There may be some comfort in hearing the shared stories of those who have been to the Underworld and not only survived to tell the tale, but returned above ground to thrive once more. It is possible, after all.

Statement of the Research Problem and Question

The Research Problem

There is some literature available on joy, happiness, and leading emotionally healthy lifestyles, as well as an abundance of research on depression and its sequelae; however, nothing could be found which addresses the precise aspect this study seeks to investigate: the pivotal moments spurring movement between the two states, what they are like, how they are experienced by individuals, what triggers such movement, and how such moments are recognized and felt as lived events by different people in different circumstances. The key focus of this research project is on the phenomenology of the lived experience of the return from the Underworld.

The Research Question

This investigation sought to explore the following question: "What is the lived experience of coming to life again after a period of emotional deadness?" Informants were asked to share their personal experiences of entering into the Underworld of grief, bereavement, and depression due to traumatic

Heidi Elowitch (Taylor)

experiences such as physical illness, loss of a loved one, divorce, rape, and so on; lingering in this state; and emerging to return to the Upperworld of feeling "alive." Participants were asked to describe their thoughts, feelings, behaviors, and actions at the various stages of their journey into the depressive spectrum and out of it to normalcy, joy, or even euphoria. The emphasis was on the experience of the turning point or transition from the Underworld to the Upperworld.

Definition of Terms

For the purposes of this study, "emotional deadness" is defined as a state of shock or numbness where one feels out of touch with life, disengaged with people, places, and things, and profoundly in despair. "Coming back to life again" is defined as the state experienced as this numbness or shock wears off and one feels engaged with people, places, and things once more. The study is specifically interested in gathering information about the transitional period between the two states. How do individual informants experience it? Is it a lived event or series of events? How is it interpreted? Is it felt in the body, intellectually, emotionally, or in some other way? "Emotional deadness" is the phrase used to convey a sense of deadness that is all but physical, encompassing dynamics of feelings, connectedness to the world, spiritual deadness, and an overall sense of lifelessness for which the English language currently has no practical term.

Tales of Awakening

CHAPTER 2
METHODOLOGY AND PROCEDURES

Research Approach

"Freud tangled the two because he was engaged in both at once: fiction and case history; and ever since then in the history of our field, they are inseparable; our case histories are a way of writing fiction" (Hillman, 1983, p. 5).

This dissertation is intended to tell a story; a case history of sorts that moves into an archetypal perspective and therefore becomes a story of healing. It is a story of synchronicity. It is based on lived experience, not fiction. It is my story and the stories of those whom I interviewed.

Predominantly viewed and processed through a Jungian lens and perspective, this research is deeply intertwined with the alchemical approach:

> Jung pointed out the prescient parallels between the individuation processand alchemy. The alchemical process is the symbolic transforming of lead into gold, where lead, denotes the metal of Saturn and gold is Sol, the new consciousness. The process occurs in stages, where the stages may require many repetitions, imagined as a circular process, endless in nature. Jung notes that this work is difficult and strewn with obstacles; the alchemical opus is dangerous. Right at the beginning you meet the "dragon," the chthonic spirit, the "devil" or, as the alchemists called it, the "blackness," the nigredo, and this encounter produces suffering. "Matter" suffers right up to the final

Heidi Elowitch (Taylor)

disappearance of the blackness; in psychological terms, the soul finds itself in the throes of melancholy, locked in a struggle with the "shadow." The mystery of the coniunctio, the central mystery of alchemy, aims precisely at the synthesis of opposites, the assimilation of the blackness, the integration of the devil. For the "awakened" Christian this is a very serious psychotic experience, for it is a confrontation with his own "shadow," with the blackness, the nigredo, which remains separate and can never be completely integrated into the human personality (Jung, 1977, p. 228). (Kiehl, 2005, "The Imaginal Realm of Depression," para. 12)

What this study's participants reported in terms of "Awakening to Life Again after a Period of Emotional Deadness" and the review of the literature on depression and recovery as well as fairy tale and myth point to a type of archetypal, universal individuation experience in those who have emerged from the Underworld:

The alchemical process mirrors the imagery of Chaos and Eros, and that of Saturn and Venus. First there is the descent into darkness, the world of shadow, where suffering is lived. The soul is struggling to find expression. For Jung the mystery of this process is in integration of the devil, the discovery and acceptance of the shadow, our personal chaos. Thus, chaos cannot be avoided, indeed the more we turn away from chaos, the stronger its pull on us. Depression is that pull into darkness, affording us the interior spatial and temporal reality to make a connection, to integrate the devil. From this dark stage of the nigredo, arises the albedo, the whitening of conscious recognition of the lived experience, but this is not the end, for what is needed to achieve transformation is embodiment. Mere conscious recognition is insufficient to give life, we need a living substance, blood, as symbolized in the rubedo, or reddening process bringing life to experiences of the world. (Kiehl, 2005, "The Imaginal Realm of Depression." para. 13)

Encompassing this work as a whole is the underlying theme of alchemy. The voyage that emotional reawakening takes one through is best exemplified by the science of alchemy. This process is a "cooking" of the soul from one state into another, so that the end product is quite different from the beginning matter. In Marie-Louise von Franz's *Alchemy: An Introduction to the Symbolism and the Psychology* (1980), she states:

> If you dream of an archetype in human form, that means you could, to some extent, incarnate it. It could manifest in you, and could express itself through you, that is the whole idea of the inner Christ. If you dream of the wise old man, then it can happen that you get into an impossible situation where you are asked an impossible question, but suddenly a perfect answer comes to you! If you are honest, you feel obliged to admit afterwards that it was not you speaking. "It" spoke through you; you could not claim to have had such a thought. That would be the wise old man manifesting in you, someone or something not identical with the ego, but helpful in a difficult situation. (p. 30)

Rilke (as cited in Dembski, 2006) feels that dark abysses are overcome through the reverie of relating, through reaching out to the world and holding the contradictions in life. Jung believed that holding the tension of opposites is critical to the individuation process and says that "the first step of this process is the descent, which is "the dread and resistance which every natural human being experiences when it comes to delving too deeply into himself; at bottom, the fear of the journey to Hades" (1937/1968, p. 336). The process that evolves is one of descent, whereby the ego is pulled into closer contact with the unconscious, where the ego faces its shadow. This is experienced as a lowering of energy from the outer world. The interior has called and the removal of attention from the outer world leads to a lowering of affect. The inner world is one of chaos, it need not follow the linear and rational way of the outer collective. Its language is imaginal (Dembski, 2006).

This passage neatly summed up my intention in stating that an alchemical underpinning supports both the autobiographical-heuristic as well as the phenomenological portions of my research. Research topics are much larger than those who investigate them. As researchers, we may claim them, but they also claim us, and what we end up saying in and through our work is both us and not us. We can take a piece of the credit for starting, exploring, and synthesizing the material, but portions of the work are also spurred, deepened, expanded, and finalized by forces outside of ourselves. These may be archetypal figures speaking through us, the result of alchemical combinations of different ingredients combined correctly and "cooked" for just the right amount of time to produce a good finished product, or a numinous aspect of the imaginal realm coming to life through the work of the research process, a labor of both love and pain.

Tales of Awakening

The freedom allowed in the style of research belonging to depth psychology and phenomenology provides a fertile breeding ground (or alchemical vessel) for bringing attention and illumination to topics, ideas, concepts, theories, and stories that may never have found expression without this framework (except maybe by increasing their shadow aspects). This openness allows for some fascinating creative work to emerge, research which has the potential to increase the richness of what is currently known and to give life to ideas not yet conceived. I am excited at the thought of being part of this process myself. I treasure the notion of having metaphorically participated in the alchemical process of gathering up material that may have seemed base, lifeless, inert, or useless on its own, and lovingly transformed it into the precious, jewel-like, final product of this dissertation. I valued the metaphoric challenge of collecting, working with, and immersing myself in the alchemical endeavor of turning disparate components of my dissertation research into a whole which is larger than the sum of its parts and will "carry the aromas of the landscapes of the heart" (R. Romanyshyn, personal communication, January, 2001).

Research Methodology

For this study, two research styles were employed. For the chapter containing this researcher's own experience of coming to life again after a period of emotional deadness, an

Heidi Elowitch (Taylor)

autobiographical heuristic component was utilized. Moustakas (1994) speaks to the relevance of heuristic inquiry:

> Heuristic research came into my life when I was searching for a word that would meaningfully encompass the process that I believed to be essential in investigations of human experience. The root meaning of *heuristic* comes from the Greek word *heuriskein* meaning to discover or find. It refers to a process of internal search through which one discovers the nature and meaning of experience and develops methods and procedures for further investigation and analysis. The self of the researcher is present throughout the process and, while understanding the phenomenon in increasing depth, the researcher also experiences growing self-awareness and self-knowledge. Heuristic processes incorporate creative self-processes and self-discoveries. (p. 17)

As the researcher, my own response to the study question was placed in a separate chapter from the participants' interviews but was analyzed along with the participants' responses as though it were a transcribed interview. Despite this unique approach, it is felt that my experience in this area will add to the richness of this investigation rather than detract from it. As Moustakas says, "the deepest currents of meaning and knowledge take place within the individual through one's senses, perceptions, beliefs, and judgments. This requires a passionate, disciplined, commitment to remain with a question intensely and continuously until it is illuminated or answered" (p. 18).

For the following chapter, I interviewed 5 participants in settings such as their homes or my office. It was anticipated that these safe and comfortable places would allow and encourage them to express their experiences fully. I audiotaped each interview, assessed it according to Giorgi's (1985) method, and followed up by allowing my participants to review the transcripts to ensure that their experiences had been fully and properly conveyed and understood.

Creswell (1998) points out that in qualitative research "the topics about which we write are emotion laden, close to the people, and practical" (p. 19), and to meet this situation "we ask open-ended research questions, wanting to listen to the participants we are studying and shaping the questions after we 'explore'" (p. 19). The topic I proposed to investigate was truly one that would be considered emotion-laden, close to the participants, and yet also imbued with great practical value. It appeared to be cathartic for people to process their traumatic moments with an interested and sympathetic listener, particularly in light of the fact that the study's thrust was to help others through the same process. It was soothing, healing, and empowering for participants to describe their individual experiences of re-engagement with life. In this regard, informants viewed their time as spent practically both for themselves and others who might benefit from their energy, effort, and courage, as a form of social service.

In a phenomenological study, the investigator enters the world of the informants with "empathy, openness, and being present for others" (Creswell, 1998, p. 31) in order to understand deeply their perception, to comprehend how they experience the phenomenon in question, and to determine what meaning it has in their lives. Interviews are then carefully transcribed and read in order to extract key comments or quotes. The meaning of these statements is condensed into themes that are described and elaborated on in the discussion section.

Epoche is the principle of bracketing out any preconceived notions that belong to the researcher by making them distinct and clear at the beginning of a study so they do not taint the outcome or the findings (Creswell, 1998, pp. 53-54). Epoche or bracketing was employed scrupulously in analyzing the data from the interviews. Epoche allowed me to include my own experience with conscious awareness of my biases and prejudices. This helped minimize unintended biased presentation of the effects on the research project. Noteworthy also is that the participants may have been providing information on an unusual or powerful topic, but the descriptions they presented were of their day-to-day living with the phenomena, supplemented by creative sources such as journaling and the observations of this researcher.

The phenomenological method of Giorgi (1985) was utilized to analyze the interviews more closely by breaking the material down into natural meaning units (NMUs) and major themes. The four-step method of taking in each transcript as a meaningful whole, identifying all the natural meaning units in each interview, transforming the NMUs into themes, and organizing the themes into an aggregate essential description was used to find the heart of the experiences, so to speak.

Creswell (1998) describes the heart of qualitative research as being one whereby

> writers agree that one undertakes qualitative research in a natural setting where the researcher is an instrument of data collection who gathers words or pictures, analyzes them intuitively, focuses on the meaning of participants, and describes a process that is expressive and persuasive in language. (p. 14)

Although the data was "examined for themes, dimensions, codes and categories" (p. 20), it also did something which makes qualitative data truly a whole that is more than just the sum of its parts: it "told a story." Creswell mentions several significant concepts of qualitative research data. These include "writing persuasively so that the reader experiences being there" (p. 21); using the participant's own language, the literary concept of "verisimilitude" (p. 21); and producing "a narrative which reflects the creativity of the writer" (p. 24). The captivating part of conducting phenomenological inquiry is that anything can emerge. One does not predict or measure any specific ingredient or variable but rather allows the freedom of open-ended questions that may lead to unknown and unforeseen destinies. In this way, informants are able to express themselves without the researcher's constraints, giving rise to new possibilities for insight, treatment, and recovery as well as ideas for further avenues of research.

Research Procedures

Procedures for Gathering Data

I proposed to use the combined methods of autobiographical heuristic research to incorporate my own story and experiences and phenomenological-case study to incorporate the lived experiences of my participants. Five informants, plus myself, were involved. In order to qualify for this study, participants had to have experienced some type of grief, loss, or bereavement stemming from events such as chronic illness, death of a spouse or close friend, rape, divorce, mental illness, drug addiction and alcoholism, or abusive interpersonal relationships, yet somehow transformed their suffering into a newfound strength and deeply profound sense of "life on the other side." Persons who voluntarily self-identified through therapy groups, 12-Step, recovery, and support groups were selected for possessing the particular quality under scrutiny: the unknown factor allowing for transformation in mourning. I posted a notice about my study topic in various locations, online as well as a hard-copy flyer (see Appendix C), with a brief description of the study, my contact information, and the specification that participation would be anonymous, confidential, and completely voluntary. Participants were informed that they would have the right to discontinue at any time they wished and that appropriate referrals would be made, if needed. Respondents who appeared still to be depressed or never to have been deeply depressed or who were in any other way poorly matched for the topic were deselected from the study. Only respondents who appeared to understand the concept of the study on a depth level and could give expression to having phenomenologically experienced the topic were included in the data analysis.

Participants were asked to engage in an audiotaped interview of their responses to the research question and were told they had approximately one hour to express themselves fully. They were informed that their interview transcripts and the subsequent themes discovered would be sent to them for review to make sure their essence was appropriately captured by this researcher, and any mistakes repaired prior to completion of the study. Participants indicated their knowledge of all of the above by signing an Informed Consent Form (see Appendix A) prior to beginning the interview process.

Procedures for Analyzing Data

The data was analyzed using Giorgi's (1985) phenomenological method, as well as Creswell's (1998) intuitive approach. The depth, Jungian, mythological, and archetypal themes introduced in the beginning of the study were revisited in the final analysis of the data. The themes that emerged were examined for depth and archetypal significance and appropriately categorized. The participant's interviews were collected and read multiple times in solitude, looking for themes, new conceptual breakthroughs, or insights each time. They were allowed to "simmer" alchemically in this researcher's mind between readings so that this researcher was able to encompass the feelings of the participants during their emotional transitions and was able to understand more deeply the personal journey each informant experienced. For accuracy, after the initial draft of the analysis was complete, this researcher re-interviewed the participants in order to confirm or disconfirm any findings.

Detailed Description of Giorgi's Method

Once descriptions were obtained, the researcher followed five steps: (a) read over each interview transcript to get a holistic sense of the informant's experience, (b) divided the material into relatively small parts, or what Giorgi (1985) calls Natural Meaning Units (NMUs), (c) transformed the NMUs into themes and psychological language, (d) synthesized the themes of each interview as well as the collective themes into aggregate essential descriptions of the experience, and (e) conducted a poststructural analysis. These steps are the core of Giorgi's method. Each of these steps can be examined in greater detail.

Reading over the informant's interview to get a holistic sense of it. The Giorgi (1985) method begins by reading over the transcript several times in order to understand fully the interview in its context as a whole.

Breaking down the description into meaningful parts. Here the researcher divides the transcript into parts Giorgi (1985) calls Natural Meaning Units (NMUs). These parts are based upon the researcher's ultimate goal of learning about the psychological meaning of an experience. Giorgi states that NMUs are constituents, not elements, because they have meaning only in a certain context. NMUs are identified on the actual transcript with a mark at each location where the researcher observes a shift in meaning. The size of an NMU can vary from a word or two to a paragraph.

Transforming the meaning units into themes expressed in psychological language. In this step of the Giorgi (1985) method, thoughtful imagination is used to group NMUs together in clusters of similar meaning. The themes of the description are grouped together and expressed by the researcher in psychological language. The researcher makes explicit what the participant has expressed implicitly. In this way, the psychological meaning of the lived experience is captured.

Synthesizing the common themes into a structural description of the experience. Here the researcher determines the structure of the lived experience being investigated (Giorgi, 1985). Using the method of free imaginative variation, the researcher looks across all the themes to see what is truly invariant about the experience being investigated. This is a holistic expression of the lived experience articulated in psychological language. Previous themes may be expressed and new themes may emerge.

The structural description consists not only of context-specific constituents but also the interrelationship between them. The structure, rather than being applicable to every experience of the phenomenon under scrutiny, depicts the general or typical experience of the phenomenon. It excludes what is highly specific and likely to be atypical to an experience. "Finally, the structure is meant to convey what is truly psychologically essential about a series of experiences of the same type" (Giorgi, as cited in Grote, 2005, p. 75).

Conducting a poststructural analysis. In this last stage, the researcher uses the structure to understand more fully the empirical data gathered about the phenomena (Giorgi, 1985). The complexity and interrelationships of the experience, including prior assumptions connected to the phenomenon being explored, can be analyzed, probed, and challenged using the structure. At this stage, the researcher aspires to develop a new understanding of the phenomenon that can be of value to the field of psychology.

Procedures for Dealing with Ethical Concerns

To maintain appropriate ethical guidelines and considerations, as the researcher, I did the following: had participants read a brief explanation of the project and sign any consent forms needed, made participants aware of their right to discontinue at any time they wished, and provided any necessary referrals as needed during the research process. To minimize the likelihood of retraumatization, the study only included participants who self-identified as already on the positive side of the journey, because that was the clinical picture I was interested in assessing.

Limitations and Delimitations of the Study

Several limitations existed in regard to this study. One is that the interviews relied largely on memory, which is well known to be unreliable at best and falsely reconstructive at its worst. Because the data collected in the interviews was mostly retrospective, a wholly accurate picture of what was occurring in participant's lives during the transitional time we were investigating may not have been acquired. Another limitation is that I did not have access to the population at large and may not have obtained the most descriptive interview material. People are often guarded about negative events they have experienced and may find it very uncomfortable opening up to someone about their troubled times. It may be almost impossible for them to put their feelings into words. Even if the informants are open and accurate, this does not guarantee that the findings can be extrapolated to the population at large. Although this study is just a piece of the puzzle, only a beginning step, it is a start in an interesting new direction for research to expand.

Heidi Elowitch (Taylor)

CHAPTER 3
THE RESEARCHER'S EXPERIENCE OF THE
PHENOMENA

In this chapter, I share my own experience of lowering into the Underworld, finding odd turning points and moments of transformation, and the relief of coming to life again in the Upperworld, forever a changed being. As previously stated in my methods section, I employed the autobiographical-heuristic method to analyze my own contribution to this study. The heuristic approach holds that the researcher's personal experience can be a vital source of information about a phenomenon and does not inherently run the risk of bias (Moustakas, 1994, p. 17). In accordance with the analysis used for the participants' interviews, the Giorgi (1985) method was employed in order to identify key themes in the material. Themes are clusters of similar meaning units grouped together to give voice to discrete psychological experiences.

Though I did not interview myself, I applied the Giorgi (1985) method of analysis to my written autobiographical-heuristic material as well as my participants' interviews. This enabled me to maintain analytic integrity, consistency, and continuity throughout the study. The following is the written autobiography of my descent into emotional deadness and my eventual return. The material is broken down into Giorgian natural meaning units (NMUs) and themes which provide greater clarity and impact due to their concise nature.

The Underworld

Sense of death: I was a corpse, a cadaver, a stiff. I was the walking dead.

Sense of nonexistence: Somehow almost no one knew it. They looked right at me, stood a foot away, and didn't smell the rotting stench of my old, withered flesh falling from my bones to reveal the lifeless marrow inside. They saw the shell and apparently it impressed them, making me feel all the more blank and invisible.

Sense of being misunderstood: There were two people who actually saw that I was dead. One of them was scared to death of me because I reminded him of his own death, which he had neatly packaged away in a corner with a bow and a tag saying "Do not open till Xmas," after which time he quickly stopped celebrating all holidays so he would never have to go open that box again.

Sense of stigmatization: He shunned and shamed me whenever he got the chance, as if decimating me could erase his own tragedy.

Sense of regression: The other embraced me as if I were a defenseless infant, as if reaching out to me, embracing me, promising to heal me and make me whole would heal the dead in him and bring him back to life as well as me. He wanted so much

Heidi Elowitch (Taylor)

to help soothe my pain because he really desperately needed to heal the pain within him. Not knowing this very clearly at the time, I waited for him to heal me. Needless to say, he gave up pretty quickly. It was, of course, an impossible task. I remember that my reaction to his noticing my deadness was my first sense of where I had actually been and where I might be able to go.

Sense of shock: I had not had any real sense of how dead I had been until I met someone who made me feel alive again. As paradoxical as it sounds, he did this by actually recognizing and naming what was wrong with me: He told me I was dead inside, and I needed someone to bring me back to life. It was such a relief. It was the first time I had had any real actual connection with another human being since my soulmate had left this world. It was the first time I felt real and in my body instead of ethereal and floating. Being seen grounded me back in myself and woke me up from a state of prolonged shock.

I hate those clichés, "You don't know where you're going if you don't know where you've been," and "You can't know happiness if you haven't known pain," but frighteningly enough, they appear to be true. It's as if when you're hysterical, someone slaps you, and you calm down and realize you were out of control.

Sense of time racing: I came back to life with the same abruptness as those scenes in *ER* and *Chicago Hope* (which were favorite TV shows of Michael's and mine) when someone yells

"Charge!" and puts the paddles on your chest to shock your heart back into beating.

The Turning Point

Sense of futility: I was having a dull, dry, lifeless day like every other day for the last year since Mike was gone from this earth, and I found myself wandering alone and directionless, like an animal separated from its herd. His leaving me behind after his overdose was like suddenly being half a person. No part of my normal daily life was normal anymore. The person I did everything with was not going to be the person I did anything with ever again. I had no idea where to start, so I just picked up the pieces and crawled through the parts that were left. Everything felt weird, awkward, clumsy, one size too big or small, somehow just not right, but I had no idea what else to do except do it. I didn't want to die or go to a mental hospital, so I just held it together and tried not to fall apart.

A savior figure; sense of hope: Then someone looked at me and saw me, I mean really *saw* me, put his hand on my scrawny chest and said, "You are dead inside and you need someone to heal you." I will never know how he knew; I only know that he did, and that moment, combined with certain others that were no accident, sparked some awakening and transformation that intervened in the disintegration and flatness I was experiencing, not only halting it, but actually shifting it in the opposite direction.

Life spark reignites: That shift allowed for renewal, growth, zest for living, and energy to be restored to a soul that had felt nothing in a very long time. It is hard to explain how I could have been numb and yet in horrific pain, experiencing no momentum and yet deteriorating; it would take a more gifted soul than I to make sense of these contradictory perceptions. I was hurtling towards the abyss yet standing still. All I knew was that I wanted to be absolutely anywhere than in the prison of my own skin. The punishment of going to sleep and waking up every day in the same body was more than I could bear.

Trapped: I wanted to escape from myself so badly, yet the only option that seemed really efficient—suicide—scared me to death. I know, I know, it's sort of funny, in a dark way.

Fear: Why be scared to die if you are already dead? It was the messiness of it all, the bother, the effort of getting something to do it with, finding a time and place, fear of pain and afterlife consequences.

Exhaustion: I was just much too tired to cope with such an exhausting and unpleasant project. There had to be an easier way.

Suicidal ideation: I had fantasies of being killed in gang crossfire. I prayed that I would be shot by the police or a sniper as I walked out my front door, or killed in a car crash, something quick and painless that didn't require any more energy on my behalf because, God knows, I had none left to give. I just wanted to depart this ugly, sad, unfair planet as quickly as humanly possible, with as little effort as possible. I used to zone out during class, imagining the giant chandeliers coming loose from the ceiling, impaling me through the head and quickly drilling into the hardwood floor. In depressive literature, I think it's called *suicidal ideation*. You bet I had it. My therapist finally got aggravated with me taking about it, but I know now that was about her inability to sit with that in the room, not about me. I was where I was, no more, no less. A therapist has to let someone be where she is and respect that she'll move from there when the time is right, not when the therapist is *ready*, which places the burden on the patient who is already suffering enough. Let's assume that the universe conspires to transform or shift a situation when the time is right. There is no other way to explain how things came together for me as they did.

I remember being trapped in a sort of dead yet living hell, because even the escape of death that I so often dreamed of was not really an escape at all. For one, I didn't really want to die. Yes, I was already dead mentally, psychologically, emotionally, and spiritually, and yet I had to drag this stupid carcass around with me wherever I had to go, because somehow the world insisted I was still alive. But it wasn't really physical death that I wanted. No. It was something very different and something no one, nowhere, no matter how smart or special or talented they were, could possibly give me.

Heidi Elowitch (Taylor)

Yearning for nonexistence: What I wanted was never to have been born, simply never to have existed, or at least somehow to cease to exist without actually dying. I was scared it would hurt. I was terrified I would have some type of conscious awareness trapped in my body after I was dead; that I would be trapped in my head as they put my body on the cold tray in the bag at the morgue; and that in the box in the ground, I would have the same feeling I have during my asthma attacks. To be cremated and destroy the shell was the only hope for setting the spirit free, but what about the time of being trapped in the oven, roasting into ashes? Clearly, physical death was not going to be any picnic. So I longed and longed for the impossible: to vanish into thin air, poof, to be gone in an instant, as if I'd never been here to begin with. The harder I wanted this to be, the more I felt I was surely in hell, because for those who are truly suicidal, suicide is an escape, and I really had no escape to cling to. I was like an animal trapped in a cage with nowhere to go for relief.

Monotony: I felt everyday as if I were just going through the motions the living go through: Get out of bed, get dressed, brush teeth, drive a car, go to work, go to school, go to the gym, and see your counselor because you have issues! It all felt so useless, so dull, so mechanical.

Lifeless: I felt like a stupid robot whose soul had left long ago. There was no blood running through my veins, I hardly ever ate, rarely slept, and if someone had hooked me up to an EKG, there most likely would have been no heartbeat on the monitor. The doctors would have looked up with puzzled expressions, holding their stethoscopes, shaking their heads, saying, "I'm sorry, she's already gone. . . ."

Alone: It was so cold, and dark, and lonely. Coming home to the big, empty, silent house was the worst. It was so hard knowing no one would ever be here when I got here, no one would ever greet me again as I came up the stairs, there would never be a dinner cooking, the TV or stereo would not be on. There would always and forevermore be just . . . nothing. No hug, no kiss, no smile. Just no. Just the absence, the huge, glaring, ugly absence of anything that ever made me feel not alone. No voice, no words, no one to talk to, no one to watch TV with or eat with or sleep next to. Just me. And I was in no state to be good company to anyone, least of all myself. I tried to stay away from home as much as possible then. I would take the corpse out early in the morning, cart it around all day, take it to NA meetings at night like I had gone to with you, I mean him, for the past 4 years, because those were the people I still felt close to and that made me feel like you were still close, or like I was still close to you, or something like that. Then I would go out with them after the meetings to eat or whatever, and take the corpse home as late at night as possible to minimize the alone time there. What was once our cozy home now felt like a freaking cavern. It was creepy. I hated it, hated being alone there. The corpse in the big hollow cave. I mean home sweet home. Ah, sarcasm. Where would I be without it?

Heightened spiritual connection: I remember right after you died I could still feel your presence very closely. I knew you were nearby and that made me feel really safe for some reason. Your mother was so worried about me, having someone drive me to the funeral and the cemetery, but I knew you wouldn't let anything bad happen to me. Wow, does that sound funny—like something really bad hadn't just happened to me! Funny ironic, not funny ha-ha.

Prolonged shock: I drove around in a daze, picking up relatives and friends, driving to the funeral home in the car you got with me, and holy shit, there you were in a casket, dead as can be. You looked like you and yet nothing like you and yet just exactly like you. All my life I have been terrified of death, dying, dead people, open caskets, and then it was you, and it was completely different because it was you, so how could I be afraid of you? How could I not see you or touch you the last possible chance before they put you in the ground? I expected something different, though I'm not exactly sure what; you were cold but maybe not that cold. I think the weirdest thing was the complete stillness, the utter lack of responsiveness. . . . I tried to hold your hand, sort of, but really it could have been a board in a suit for all the energy you directed outward. I was glad you had things in your coffin that meant something to you: flowers, pictures of the family, stuffed animals, your CTR ring. I was glad I had your teddy bear and your wedding band. I kept trying to piece together the facts that the alive Michael and the spirit Michael I could feel and the object in the box were all sort of the same and sort of different, and it mostly just didn't make a whole lot of sense, but it was sort of OKAY then, because I was sort of in a fog anyway.

Distraction through action: I had conversations with crying people whose names I cannot remember. I made flyers and went to NA meetings to spread the news so your friends could come pay their respects. I remember showing up at the Tuesday night speaker meeting where one of your former sponsors was leading the meeting. He turned around and looked at me and asked, "So it's true?" I hysterically fell apart, wondering how anyone had already heard so fast. I did not shed one tear at your funeral.

Self-hatred: I wondered what the fuck was wrong with me. What kind of a frozen unfeeling bitch doesn't cry, can't cry, at her own fiancé's funeral, for God's sake? Wasn't I human? It never occurred to me that I was in shock and functioning on auto-pilot. That I had just suffered the worst trauma a person can suffer, one with a statistically worse outcome than losing even a child. I said the Serenity Prayer at your grave site after Nancy sang Fleetwood Mac's "Songbird," and we watched you disappear into the earth, covered in flowers.

Heidi Elowitch (Taylor)

We went back to your parents' house, and I wanted to get as close as possible to your ex-girlfriend/ex-fiancée. Rather than feeling jealous or competitive, I felt like she was the only person who could imagine where I was at internally, although maybe to a lesser degree. Veronica and I sat right next to each other on your bed in your room, with a photo album across our laps, sharing stories. We had never met before. She was beautiful. I wanted to hold her baby son. He looked like a child we might have had if we had ever had kids. Which we didn't. We didn't want kids, but for some reason, looking at Veronica's baby made me sad and made me want to cry. Lost opportunity or something like that. Not having a piece of something to hold onto. Nothing left of you still living? I really don't know. She was very nice to me. I was jealous that she had a husband and a baby and a complete family and a full life after you, and I had . . . shreds.

Damaged goods: So you've been gone for over 2 years now, and I still feel like a partial person, half a person, a broken piece of something that used to be whole when it was together.

Aching emptiness: I keep trying to find something, anything, to fill that broken, empty space, but nothing fixes it or makes it feel okay anymore. Not another person, not an activity or a hobby (The gym! Karate! Spanish! Sign Language! School! Work! Guys! Program! Food! The Computer!), and certainly not drugs or alcohol, since that is what killed you. I'm really pretty damn proficient at finding a million and one temporary distractions to occupy my time and energy, but at night I still have to come home to that deathly quiet, strangely empty house that you used to enliven with your smile and your warmth and just sit there with . . . me. The vacuum of empty space is enough to make anyone go insane.

Pining: It's very strange to live in the aftermath of the death of someone you love. I feel cheated by the universe out of the life I was supposed to have. I feel like the universe cheated you out of the life you were supposed to have. Of course, that means we were robbed of the life we were supposed to have. I try to picture what it would have been like, but I end up picturing what it was, and what it was would have been good enough; actually, it would have been just great without the Goddamn addiction.

Confusion: How can one problem so totally and completely eradicate the goodness of a person's soul and character? I'll never really understand the way that works, how somewhere deep down inside you, you couldn't just pull it together. Other people have done it, why couldn't you? Was it that you couldn't, wouldn't, or both?

Anger: I think I'll always be a little bit angry with you for that part in it. The feeling that you did it to yourself, that it didn't have to be this way, that you chose to die.   Blame: You could have tried harder to live, but you just gave up and left me behind to deal with the shit. I didn't deserve this on top of everything else we went through. Life wasn't fair to either one of us, it's true, but you weren't fair to me in your death, either. It's unpleasant to miss you and be mad at you at the same time. I wish I could just miss you sometimes, y'know? It would be easier and less confusing.

It annoys me greatly that everyone from friends to family to professionals to strangers think I do drugs or have an eating disorder because I lost weight after you died. How can they not realize that the living dead don't need to eat the same way they do? There isn't the same kind of body to run anymore. We don't need calories to sustain expenditures of joy, happiness, surprise, relaxation, or anything pleasant. I myself spent most of my time sleeping, including through my second year of doctoral classes. My patients, I know, will be thrilled. My professors certainly were. Actually, most were kind and understanding, but one was anything but. My mere corpselike presence both angered and frightened him, though I could never tell which one more. I wanted to explain to everybody that those of us left behind suffer from a disorder you won't find in the *DSM-IV-TR* (DSM, 2000): *Griefarexia*, the utter lack of enjoyment in food or desire to cook or eat alone. I could and still can manage to find my appetite and taste buds when I'm around others in a social setting, but alone in our house, food preparation has never advanced beyond cereal since you died, and it has to be a pretty gnarly hunger pain to get me to break out the inconvenience of bowl, spoon, box, carton. Cooking in this house was only fun when I could come home to you baking cookies or hear you preparing some wonderful casserole or homemade spaghetti sauce while you let me do my homework upstairs. You always took care of the homey things so I could keep focused on my schoolwork. You made it possible for me to keep moving ahead, and you never resented playing house-husband, doing the cooking, cleaning, dishes, plus the garden and yard work, detailing the cars and keeping the garage looking presentable, and constantly fixing the computers. I never knew just how much you did until you weren't here to do it anymore. You are the only person I know who could fix a carburetor and make a cheesecake. We would eat and watch our favorite shows together while snuggling under blankets on the couch. Now I eat alone at the kitchen table. I won't even try to replicate what I lost because the attempt would be so pathetic and unbearable. Better not to try at all.

Recurring traumatization: Today I had another one of those annoying jolts where an older widowed woman told me I really needed to "get on with it, get over it," move on with my life, blah, blah, blahhhhhhh, because I am "young . . . ." It's not the first time I've heard it and it's not the first time I've heard it from her. If I had a dollar for all the useless instructions I've been given on how to cope with my loss, I'd be rich. Until I had my loss, I had no idea there were special grieving instructions with a time limit included for the young. Who knew? No mourning too long, or too much, or too publicly, or for the wrong person, certainly not a drug addict! Why, he as much as asked for it!

Shame: But who knew they would think that of me? That by being with the "wrong type of person" I'd as much as asked for it? *Well, you knew it could happen. . . .* Excuse me, but I kind of thought death was one of those things that could happen to anyone: cancer, traffic accident, stray bullet, mugging, banana peel. *Well, but what he was doing increased the odds. . . .* Um, fire fighter, police officer, tow truck driver, soldier, surfing enthusiast? What they were subtly—and not really so subtly—implying was that he deserved it because he was doing illicit and immoral things, things against the laws of nature and society that "good" citizens follow and uphold, and so he had it coming. And so did I, because I had chosen those immoral and illegal activities by association, by choosing to stay with him. We were just two doomed individuals, waiting for our comeuppance. It was staggeringly gross to live through the stigma of being an overdosed addict's left-behind girlfriend. When I would tell people my fiancé had passed away, their faces would contort in anguish. *Oh, what from?* I always answered truthfully "a drug overdose." I was determined to help Mike carry his 12-step cause after his death by reducing the stigma, secrecy, and shame surrounding it. People's faces would always perceptibly change and lose a noticeable bit of compassion and empathy when they heard the cause, and you could see they considered it something blameworthy, not accidental, something he could be held responsible for. It was always a real pick-me-up for me, the survivor. The only people whose faces grew even sadder and more empathic were those in 12-step circles, because they *knew*: there but for the grace of God go I.

Today, I saw a friend from our past. It was poignant and bittersweet to be able to talk about you with someone who actually knew you and remembered you from when you were still alive. It's hard to believe, but you have been gone (and I say gone because for a millisecond it sounds easier than *dead*) for so long now that I find myself talking about you more often than not to people who never met you, never knew you, don't know how you looked, spoke, acted, behaved, what kind of person you were, nothing. Your name, angel, has become *My Fiancé Who Died.* What a horrible way to have to refer to someone, and yet, what else do I say that means anything to anyone else?

You have become some kind of living memorial to my group home and continuation school kids: *Don't Do This.* An anti-crack testimonial. I carry the message for those who cannot, blah, blah, blah, and I know it's supposed to be important and lifesaving work, but sometimes I feel like a boring, droning broken record and like I'm not really getting through to anyone or piercing these kids souls, because they don't have a real person to attach to the story. How different it would have been if you had stayed in recovery and you had gone into these schools and group homes

Heidi Elowitch (Taylor)

(Hospitals and Institutions! Hospitals and Institutions!) and talked to the kids face-to-face about your abuse, about being molested, getting into drugs to numb the pain, becoming addicted, the hardships of attempting to quit, and life at the bottom of a cesspool. I hate that it comes secondhand through me. I never wanted to be your spokesperson.

Recurrent pain: Today the pain of being alone and alive in this world was once again very nearly more than I could take, and I would say I *almost* cracked, except for the fact that I did crack. I was driving to work, of course, right past the cemetery (big surprise), and the hideous and grotesque vomiting of emotional sludge that I can't seem to find the bottom of came over me yet again. I feel like a bulimic, yet I can't seem to remember when I binged on this rotting and foul mess or why I would have done so. Why wasn't someone there to stop me? Why not God? The intensity of the emotional pain was, as it always is, unbearable. I stifled it for as long as I could, and then I let it out slowly, tears rolling down my face while cruising through traffic, a regular habit since the week you left.

Depersonalization: I was making weird animal sounds, which made me cry even more because I felt sympathy for someone who sounded so agonized, like it wasn't even me. I thought I would die right then and there, or maybe I just wished I would. Either way, as they would say in 12-step programs, I prayed to "surrender."

Tales of Awakening

Surrender: I fell to my knees—figuratively, since I was still driving—and prayed so freaking hard to God he had to hear me this time. I begged like no tomorrow for the pain to be lifted or transformed into something bearable, something tolerable, something I could live with. I waited what seemed like hours of eternity but was maybe 15 minutes, and for the first time that I ever prayed for help, the pain lifted. It was a bona fide miracle, and I am truly grateful for that moment's relative peace.

No respite, however well-deserved, is ever granted for long, though. The pain comes back in smaller or larger doses, depending on the events of the day.

Awkwardness: Always in the background is the oddness of having to include your absence into conversation. Today, meeting someone new at the dog park, there was the spitting image of you: your height, your build, although a little thinner, your style of dress, even wearing one of those silly hats you had on in that picture your parents have up of you bar-be-cueing in their backyard. It was so bizarre all I could do was stare and tell Scott, "If you ever want to know what Michael looked like. . . ." It was really freaking me out. I feel like I say, "My dead ex-boyfriend" or "My fiancé who died" about once a day, and you've been dead for 2 ½ years. When will I not have to talk about it anymore?

My deadness defines me: When will it not need to be part of a conversation with every new person in order somehow to

Heidi Elowitch (Taylor)

explain who *I am* today? It feels like I carry a ghost around with me that no one else can see but I can always sense is there, and I must explain it before others sense it and wonder what is wrong with me.

Losing tangibility: The space between the living and the dead is very thin and very hard to cross. This doesn't really make any sense to me, and I find it frustrating and hurtful. I have felt your presence so close to me sometimes since you've been gone, and other times, it feels like you never really existed at all except as a figment of my imagination, and those are the times I feel very guilty. It's starting to happen more and more that I feel detached from what it was like to be with you, to love you, to be in love with you, and I can't recall my attachment to the lost object.

Self-blame, judgment: Does this make me a bad widow? Does this happen to other people who have lost a loved one? It sounds base and mean, but it's weird how there are times when I can go to the cemetery and feel nothing and times when I can go and cry my eyes out without making it through a 12-step prayer. It makes me feel like I'm schizophrenic.

Sometimes I have to go look at the pictures on the wall or consciously meditate on specific good times we had, events with friends or something funny you did in the house. . . . I actually have to run the tape in my head to remember what our life was like back when you were alive, and it feels like someone else's life. I find it hard to attach my soul to the good memories. They seem hollow and painful now, like rusted out old metal that might scratch you and give you tetanus if you pick it up. One image still makes me smile. I remember being on the phone with my grandparents and you were still sleeping, but when you woke up and started coming downstairs, you were crawling on all fours like a gorilla making these silly faces through the railing of the stairs. For some reason that slice, that image still creates lightness, I think because it captures your playfulness and who you truly were when you weren't haunted by darkness. When the drugs took over, or the urge to use them, you were one of the ugliest people I ever knew. You created so much pain for so many people, it's still hard to reconcile that you were the same person and not two different souls living in one body. But maybe you were.

I thought my life was going to consist of writing a dissertation on chronic pain and illness featuring you as a participant, helping me through the process by supporting me in life while I had to be a crazy doctoral student. The next thing I know, I'm a crazy doctoral student alone and you are the focus of my dissertation in an entirely different and really sad way.

Blindsided: I never saw it coming, like a truck that collided with me head on at full speed, forever changing the course and direction of my life, sending me reeling in a direction in which I never expressed an interest in traveling. Quite the contrary, I probably made it clear that I was more than worried about going there on numerous occasions. Life has a way of handing some people their greatest nightmares and other people their greatest wishes. Greetings from one of the less fortunate ones.

So I went out to the cemetery one of the days around Christmas and left what was left of a battered poinsettia out there. It was already dark because I'm working a lot now, trying really hard to move ahead with my life and finish school and what not, and it's winter and we're off of daylight savings time. The drive out to the darkened graveyard was desolate and creepy.

Ambivalence: It was so dismal, and part of me wanted to turn the car around and just not bother, but part of me felt dutiful and obligated to make the appearance and the gesture. So I kept going, making my way almost more by radar than by sight. Finally, I was far from the freeway and along the back part of the dirt road that leads along the mountain. I parked the car and walked through the headstones with a flashlight until I found yours, put the plant down and said "Bye, Babe," and jumped back into the car with a shiver.

Confusion: It was probably my shortest stay out there, but it was dark and cold, and I just didn't feel comfortable. Part of me felt relieved to leave, and part of me felt ashamed and guilty for being relieved. Do we ever get this grief thing right?

Living life forward for the deceased: My gift to you in your death was supposed to be to carry the message for you because you could no longer carry it for yourself. So after you died, especially the first year, I lived in 12-step meetings. I was there several times a week and, later on, several times a month, sharing your story in the hope of keeping someone else alive. As time passed, and my life started to become about other things, Thank God, I didn't really feel the need to go to meetings so much anymore. But I have tried at least to go on the anniversary of your death. It's the gift that keeps on giving—how sick is that?

Finding a meaning in the tragedy: The gift of dying promotes the message of the necessity of recovery to other addicts...Every year, I share the same message that my sponsor told me right after you died: "Some die so that others may live, because if people didn't see people dying from this disease, no one would be compelled to quit." Usually, I don't get a very big response, other than people telling me they're sorry for my loss, sorry about what happened to you. This year, however, something really weird happened. Almost every single person in the room shared that they had lost someone to the disease of addiction, too. Literally, almost each person in attendance at that particular meeting had lost a brother, a spouse, a daughter, a friend. It was pretty overwhelming to have that much loss and death contained in a room that small.

Group identification: We all just looked at each other with the mask of the marked: "I know." And then we smiled that grimace of a smile that isn't really a smile, but you do it anyway when you look at the face of another survivor.

Heidi Elowitch (Taylor)

The Transformation

Pathetic fate: Sometimes I feel so strong compared to the person I was when you were alive, it's almost as if I'm glad you died, because I don't know if I'd be who I am now if you'd continued to live. I don't know if it would have ever given me enough room, enough breathing space to change, and then I wonder if this is what I mean by "Everything happens for a reason, there is a reason for everything that happens, and we are all exactly where we are, experiencing what we are supposed to be experiencing, when we are experiencing it," my little mantra that helps me make sense of everything that has happened in my life and helps me let go without having to know why and helps me to counsel others who want answers when there aren't any except what we can create out of the experience ourselves as we endure it, live in it, live through it, soak in it, alchemically alter into something else from the process, to transform into something else, whatever we were meant to be, to become.

Survivor guilt: I still can't feel those feelings without wondering if I should feel guilty for thinking such thoughts, or wondering if I am really terrible for not feeling guilty, because sometimes I don't. Then I wonder if this would ever make sense to anyone but me, and that used to feel isolating, but now it's okay. Being different isn't necessarily a bad thing. I guess I've not only adjusted but maybe learned to cherish what makes me distinctly unique. And there I go again; is it okay to feel good about being a survivor of someone's death? I think it has to be.

The unfillable absence: So, I had surgery again yesterday for the third time since you're not here anymore. No one takes care of me the way you did; no one else even comes close. There hasn't been a time that I've set foot in a doctor's office or a hospital since you've died that it hasn't been a bitter experience dealing with pain and suffering in your absence. My head ruminates with cellular level memories of what it was like when I had to go through those things "and Mikey was here."

You were almost always with me, but the most important part of that was that when you were with me you were really WITH me. You were completely and totally present, 100% in the moment, going through the experience and the process with me, no matter how miserable it might be. And you went through it with kindness and a cheerful, positive attitude, filled with love, caring, nurturing, and fondness that you were able to demonstrate easily and openly. You never held anything back, I never had to wonder if you really cared or if you were really sincere or if you really wanted to be there for me, because every nuance about you from your voice to your touch to your actions made it beyond evident that there was nowhere else you would want to be.

I remember you coming into the pre-op rooms when they had trouble putting in my IVs, holding my hands, and talking softly to help calm me down because I was hysterical after their

Heidi Elowitch (Taylor)

fourth botched attempt. I saw anguish and concern all over your face. You would insist on being let into the recovery room as soon as possible to be there when I came out of anesthesia, introducing yourself as my fiancé, not just because it would get you in easier, but because that's who you were proud to be. You would stroke my hair and face and hold the juice for me after putting the straw in. You didn't want me to strain myself or stress myself one bit; you wanted to take care of me as much as you could. I felt safe and loved when you were around. When we went home, you would help me take a bath, you would cook for me . . . homemade chicken soup or pasta, whatever I wanted. You never acted as if you were going out of your way or as if it was a burden.

No substitute for the deceased: The first person I dated after you were gone was very similar in his ability to be nurturing and care-taking in the hospital setting, coming into recovery and stroking my face and hair, holding my juice, but spent the pre-op time on his lap-top playing computer games. After spending one night with me, he took off to go have a "night out with the boys" because, in a classic statement I will never forget, he "didn't see no ring on this finger." Rude awakening number 4,012 or so, I seem to have lost count somewhere along the line. You always took off work to be with me for medical issues, even if it was just a doctor's appointment, saying that you had a family issue that came first, but everyone who came after you had work as their priority, a human being (me) second. The third guy had to finish washing a car first while I was in the ER, and the fourth guy was sure to let me know "Mondays and Fridays are hard days to get off work" and acted like he was picking up a sack of potatoes when I came out of surgery, writhing in pain.

Hope against hope: Then there's that gut-wrenching anticipatory hope every time the phone rings, even though common sense and brute logic tells me plain as day it's not going to be you on that phone. And still, amazingly, the lurching disappointment when the inevitable is confirmed, and the immediate wave of nauseating guilt for whoever was thoughtful enough to give me a call, not knowing their appearance on my line caused me an extra pinch of daily let down. Crazy, isn't it? Everything is ugly now. Colorless, tasteless, silent, numb. Except for when it hurts.

Hanging on by a thread: December 29, 2006 was the 4-year anniversary of your death. We went out to the cemetery with yellow and red roses and a tiny Christmas tree and said prayers and talked to you. Later, I can never remember about what. The prayers are always the same: the few 12-step prayers I know by heart, and a lot of wishing that you are in a good place and also able to be there to meet and take care of everyone who has died after you, and prayers for those who are sick or suffering from addiction not to have to join you yet. The people with me usually become more teary-eyed and choked up than I do. In fact, I have a hard time recalling being able to feel much in the way of emotion at your grave ever. I know it is your resting place, and I hate seeing it empty and unkempt; I feel good about bringing flowers and plants and cleaning the dirt and grass off your stone as a way of taking care of you even after you are dead. I like it to look dignified and cared for, to announce that you have not been forgotten or abandoned by the world and those who cared for you when you walked among us. Yet crying eludes me.

Abandonment anger: I often feel empty, frequently still angry and annoyed at you for leaving: leaving me, our family and friends, this world, this life. We, they, I, it needed you here and still do, and it pisses me off that you left so early. That's my signal that I've been at your grave long enough, and it's time for me to gather up my thoughts, items, visitors, and go. I can only take certain doses. I always kiss my fingertips and touch them to your gravestone before I leave. It's the only way I can kiss you goodbye now, and it feels wrong and strange to leave without kissing you goodbye. We always did in real life, waking and walking and talking life. I don't want to walk away without a goodbye kiss now anymore than I did then.

Despite all the aforementioned, the cemetery is still not a place where I feel your presence strongly. Rather, it still clouds our house like a dark cavernous cave that never warms up, never gets enough sun or daylight, always feels damp and dismal. When you left you took all the warmth and light right out of the house with you and nothing has brought it back so far, not cleaning, not prayers and blessings, not burning candles or incense, not opening all the blinds and trying to let as much sunlight flow in as possible, not playing music, not opening the windows up to let the breeze flow through, not having pets and live animals present. There remains a certain chill, an odd coldness and unsettling quietness to this house that makes it hard to stay here for too long a stretch of time. The intense emptiness and stultifying quietness is enough to make one go crazy after a while. There is no one to talk to, to look at, to hold, to be held by, to laugh with, to get a hug from after a hard day at work, to have a meal with, to share anything with at all. It reminds me of one of those psychology questions that is supposed to be indicative of one's attitude toward death: "If you found yourself in a room with four walls, a floor, a ceiling, no windows or doors, and you were all alone, how would you feel?" I was always awed by hearing people respond "peaceful," "relaxed," "safe," "meditative." My first reaction was always a gut-wrenching terror: "Trapped!" followed by "cold," "lonely," "scared." And here I am.

The dead as a guide/my own personal Persephone: So this year, on the 29th, we were remembering that you had been gone for 4 years. The very next day, the 30th, my friend's brother died unexpectedly. He was only 25 years old; you had been 27 when you left us. It was eerily more than coincidental. I didn't know what to think. I immediately prayed for you to be there to greet him, to welcome him, to show him the way so he wouldn't be scared or get lost, so he would have a friend right away on the other side. I realize as I write this that it must sound crazy to other people. But that's what I always do when I hear that someone is sick, or suffering, or gone. I think of you and how you might have gone before them to make it easier for them somehow, someway. I know it's weird.

So there we were, trying to celebrate Christmas, and remember you, and then the next thing you know, it was 2002 all over again. Another young man was gone the very next day and there I was, sitting at another memorial in a church filled with crying people. I honestly have no idea if I'd been in a church since you left, though I'm sure I must have been. Everything surrounding that is foggy. When they did the photo montage of his life from a baby, to a child, they must have wondered who the hell I was. The next day there was a viewing, and the funeral. Funeral, family, friends, fiancé, flowers, finality. I never noticed how many sad things surrounding death start with f. It was beyond surreal.

Now I'm clairvoyant: I hugged his girlfriend and whispered to her "No one can understand unless they've been there." Poor girl was like "Thanks, but who on earth are you?" Bizarre how I felt the insta-bond of loss with a perfect stranger. I sat across from her and watched her face as one shade of anguish after another passed over it when they lowered the casket into the ground. I knew every tortured sound that came from watching a box containing the body of the person you thought you were going

Tales of Awakening

to spend the rest of your life with disappear into the ground. When people asked me what it was like being there, I said it was like sitting through Mike's events from 4 years ago, only being able to feel everything this time. I felt the parents' loss of their son, my friends' loss of their sibling, and most exquisitely his fiancé's loss of . . . everything.

Holidays stink: Funny how I've really grown to hate this time of year. It's supposed to be the most festive, the most cheerful, the fun and family-oriented joyous holiday blah, blah, blah. Shopping, presents, wrapping gifts, parties, cooking, vacations, and travel. To me it's so unbearably dry and bleak, so cold and gray, so wet and unforgiving. The wind makes my tiny frame feel like I'm going to be blown away like Dorothy in *The Wizard of Oz*, my feet barely sticking to the ground as I walk from place to place, head down, arms crossed, breath held. It's dark late in the morning and early in the afternoon, and I am tired all the time. The emotionally jolting rollercoaster starts its yanking zigzag—the holidays, your death anniversary, New Year's Eve, today would-have-been-your-birthday, Valentine's Day is for lovers!! Usually, a nice romantic break-up falls somewhere in the midst of that crazy time when I get to figure out if I'm invited anywhere at all for anything and whose house I get to be the orphan at this year. Have I mentioned how much I look forward to spring and summer when all this feels a million miles behind me? Maybe not yet.

Preview déjà vu: Today, I was going through some old school papers, and I found an essay I wrote before you died. Talk about crazy. Talk about a premonition. Talk about weird. So here it is:

It is difficult to sum up in a short paper the impact that this book had on me emotionally. I found it very powerful and tremendously touching. I read this book immediately after coming home from the hospital while recuperating from a painful surgery, so the experience of reading this work was particularly poignant for me. I truly feel that this is the best work I have ever read on loss, grief, depression, and recovery, because it speaks from and to the heart rather than the head. This book will resonate with me for a long time. [The book was Robert Romanyshyn's (1999) *The Soul In Grief: Love, Death, and Transformation*. I would love to think someday someone will feel that way about *this* book].

My two biggest fears in life are the thought of my own death and the thought of losing my partner. I don't know exactly why I have such a crippling fear of my own death, other than the fear of the unknown and my familiarity with pain and illness. I have always heard it said that losing a child is the hardest loss to bear; I do not have children, but I have always thought that as tragic and awful as that would be, it would be harder still to lose a spouse. People usually expect their children to grow up, move out

Tales of Awakening

of the house, and form families of their own. No one expects to lose a partner—they plan to grow old together and be there to love and support one another through life's adversities and joyous times. The profound aloneness one would feel from this loss is staggering and almost incomprehensible. [Who knew!]

Oddly, in addition to the fact that I was in a sad mood from my surgery, I suffered the abrupt ending of a 3-year relationship with my significant other about a week after finishing the book. My fiancé relapsed after being in recovery from addiction for some time, and our relationship shattered virtually overnight. I could not compare this loss to the death of a longtime spouse, but it certainly was traumatizing and shadowed some of the feelings detailed in the book. I felt lost, terribly alone, scared, numb, shocked, depressed, anxious, lonely, and stunned. Even now the ugly events of that night and its aftermath seem surreal. There are times when I feel nothing at all, and the next moment, I'm sobbing. I thought it was an odd synchronicity that I would be in that state after reading about it in the book. In a way, I think it was fortunate that I had read the work right beforehand, because I feel it helped me to cope. It made me remember that other people have endured far greater tragedies and have come through on the other side [eerie!] to find happiness and enjoyment once more in life. I guess you could say the book got me out of my own head and also gave me strength and hope.

On page five, the book states: "In the midst of loss I was encouraged by well-meaning and good-intentioned friends to get back into the swing of things" (Romanyshyn, 1999, p. 5). I was surprised that people reacted to me and my loss in the same way. I was told "Get over it," "It's a blessing," "So what?" and "You should have expected this." [The same things they said when you died]. Friends who have gone through their own losses, pain, and suffering could not tolerate watching me go through mine. I felt like I had to put on a mask and discuss only irrelevant issues, or risk being shunned like a leper because my grief was [and still is] so frightening and intimidating to others. It magnifies the aloneness a hundredfold.

I have found that most others do not understand or comprehend the way in which I wish to deal with my separation and loss. As an individual with chronic illness, I have what is dauntingly referred to in the field as "a sense of a foreshortened future." I have always had the uncomfortable but useful intuition that we will not be here forever, and therefore I do not want to leave things ugly or left unsaid today that I may regret tomorrow. I also have some time in 12-step programs such as Al-Anon that have taught me to "keep my side of the street clean." I cannot account for anyone else's side of the street, just my own. So the fact that I want to keep things human and decent with people who matter to me, even if they have hurt me or let me down, seems to disturb people immensely. I just don't have time to be filled with hatred; life is too short. I need to do what feels right for me in the time I have allotted, for to do otherwise would be a betrayal of my spirit and soul.

I lost my grandfather when I was a child, and my aunt a few years ago, one to a heart attack and the other to cancer. In between these two relatives, five friends either died or were killed between the time I was 13 and 21 years old. Many of these were brutal and harsh deaths; hit and run drivers, gang crossfire, motorcycle and car accidents, and overdoses. In an eerie synchronicity to the book, my grandfather's death from a heart attack took place at a holiday dinner right in front of my grandmother as well as their closest friends. My aunt who died was the child of these grandparents. I often marvel at my grandmother, who has had to survive the deaths of her spouse and her child; I cannot imagine what has gotten her through these events intact. My heart grieves for her, not only for these losses, but because she never did find happiness or another companion again. She is one of the bravest people I know. I wish I could tell her that, but one of the ways she has held herself together is by maintaining a certain brittleness that I respect and do not want to shatter.

I am only 33 years old, and sometimes I find it hard to believe how much grief [!] I have already experienced. Sometimes

I feel scared about what else will happen in the future; most of the time I try to be thankful and grateful for the time I do have to live and be with my friends and loved ones. What else is there to do in this fragile place we call life?

Well, if that wasn't eerie enough on its own, it comes with a paper I wrote about the oddity of the house and its contents after you moved out, but were still very much alive. For all the world, it sounds like you are already dead. When I look at it now, it makes me think the universe was preparing me long before you actually left. I probably would not have been able to live through the shock otherwise. So here goes Fortune Telling, Part Two:

There are parts of Robert Romanyshyn's (2001) *Mirror and Metaphor* which correspond to ideas in *The Soul in Grief* (1999) and also to the events I described in my current state of being as well as my recent past. Mention is made of the way in which time and space are experienced differently in different rooms of the house, and how we live differently in these places for that very reason (Romanyshyn, 2001, p. 51). He goes on to describe how the different items in each room conjure up varying feelings and memories. I have felt this truth palpably in my own house. There is nowhere I can go where I am not reminded of a time spent together, a moment shared, or an event that happened. The kitchen is where we used to cook, the living room is where we used to eat and watch TV, the office is where we used to work together, and the bedroom is where we used to sleep next to each other. The belongings in each location are further reminders of gifts we were given, items we picked out together, or things placed in certain ways while we were decorating our new home together. These things shout at me to look at them while I struggle to look away. They haunt me and taunt me, while I do my best to pretend they are not there, for it is too painful to see them right now. Photographs of happier times try to catch my attention, while I attempt to go through the house with blinders on. It took me a whole month to spend time anywhere in the house besides my bed. That is because the house and the things in it contained and continue to sustain my psychological life. As long as psychological life can be captured and stored in material objects as well as my heart and head, there is apparently no escape. I wish I had a rented apartment where I could give 30 days notice and leave it all behind.

The moments in which the window of separation between self and other, between person and world, between logic and soul are broken are the moments of great joy and great sorrow. These are the only occasions powerful enough to break through the walls that normally separate us from other people, the world, and our spiritual lives. How I futilely wish that we could grow only in joy and never in sorrow.

The experience of restored connection is that moment when we suddenly come to life again [Here I very nearly fall out of my chair! I had my dissertation topic before you died??? Before

I knew my topic changed? And they say you don't choose your topic, your topic chooses you, but this is just too weird for words. This is creepy weird.] after a blow to the heart and soul; when we suddenly experience hunger, thirst, and energy after a long period of numbness and slumber. [Oh, I don't know, one might call it, say, emotional deadness]. It is the spark of caring anew about ourselves [say, coming alive again . . . somebody stop me here] when we had stopped and the realization that we have begun caring for another when we never thought we would again. It is the desire to live once more when we only wanted to fade away and quietly cease to exist. Mostly, it is the realization that we are still somehow alive when we thought that the biggest part of us had died. [I am now officially going to keel over.]

The experience of restored connection changes how we are present in the world by making us acutely aware of life's fragility and its preciousness. It makes us much more careful and cautious with the time we have with ourselves and with others. It allows us to know the world more fully and more honestly. We know things as they truly are and no longer just as we wish them to be. It allows us a second chance to do things the way we would have the first time around, if only we had known then what we know now.

So now it is over 6 years since I resided in the Underworld and came back to life in the Upperworld and found out that, indeed, it is not a onetime journey, not an E-ticket ride at

Tales of Awakening

Disneyland, but a deeply sobering rollercoaster we go into and out of many times. The Underworld is one hell of a place to survive, pun intended.

The Upperworld

This December 29th, 2009 will mark the 7th year of your passing on. It is really hard to believe that rather than this July 14th being our 6-year wedding anniversary, it is instead almost a decade that you have been dead. It has been difficult to be completely in the Upperworld since I have been devoted to a project about you, the Underworld, what happened to me after you died, other people's journey's in and out of the dark places, and my getting thrown back in there myself. I imagine that is how it was intended to be for some reason. Maybe because I hadn't fully finished my alchemical process, and I needed more cooking. Who knows? Certainly not me.

I am hoping the end of this project allows some healing and closure, for both of us, and that I will be able to move on in a good way. It's hard to do that when something is still the focus of your life's major work. I think it will be good to let go, now that I've done the work I feel I was meant to do or intended to do for whatever reason. It's time for some whitening and gold after all that red and black, alchemically speaking. Choose the right, baby, choose the right. Time to breathe again.

CHAPTER 4
PRESENTATION OF FINDINGS

Overview

To explore the experience of coming to life again after a period of emotional deadness, as the researcher, I interviewed five participants who agreed to share their experience of the phenomenon in question. In interviews which lasted approximately 1 hour, the participants shared their experiences of coming to life again after periods of emotional deadness. The interview question was simply the single open-ended question: "What is your lived experience of coming to life again after a period of emotional deadness?" The participants were asked to answer the question as fully as possible, while I listened attentively, intervening only if something was unclear. All of the participants prefaced their responses by explaining how they arrived in the Underworld and what that was like, before noting their transition to the Upperworld and how they experienced that turning point.

It was strikingly difficult to listen to some of the participants' experiences and to read through their transcripts repeatedly. As a researcher and a psychologist, I was struck by the moments of sorrow I felt hearing and reading about the life-altering experiences the informants had been through. I was equally surprised by the incredible strength and resiliency demonstrated by individuals in crisis, and by their ability to find meaning in their struggles, including being appreciative of them. This chapter provides a brief descriptions of the participants and the themes gathered in their interviews. Chapter 5 explores the themes common to all the participant interviews, provides a structural description of the experience of coming to life again after a period of emotional deadness, and relates experience to common themes in fairy tale and mythology. Chapter 6 summarizes the material, discusses implications for clinical and depth psychology, and offers suggestions for further research and treatment.

Susannah

My first interview was with Susannah, a 43-year-old Caucasian female who was in the early stages of the recovery process from drug and alcohol addiction and was working a 12-step program. She was eager to participate in the interview and talk about her experiences. I asked her about her enthusiasm, given that she would be recalling some of her darkest moments. She said she hoped that her interview and my research would help someone and that talking about it helped her to see what she had come through. Twenty-five themes emerged in Susannah's interview, all of which she confirmed upon my sharing them with her after analyzing the transcript. The Underworld journey as a path of deep and unbearable pain, increased spiritual connections, and loving forgiveness for self and others were major themes for Susannah.

Following are Susannah's themes, each illustrated by natural meaning units (NMUs) from her interview:

The Underworld

Complete emptiness/unbearable pain: Understanding you are completely empty, only knowing the feeling of sadness becomes too much to bear.

Suicidal ideation: Mostly, I found to get over rape and allow yourself to feel it, be prepared for pain so deep you feel like taking your own life.

Loss of a loved one: The hardest is coming to terms about someone you love taking their own life. That isn't supposed to happen.

Emotional deadness: No wonder I was dead. How would you like to feel this?

Terrifying/terrible experiences/life-altering trauma: How quickly I forget the times my Bi-polar Disorder drove me down to the brink of total insanity. Being a survivor of rape, suicide of a husband—widow—drug addiction, mental illness—bi-polar—co-dependency that continues to ruin my life.

I was told I had Bi-polar when I turned 17 years old. I went into my first of many mental hospitals. I became very sick. I went into a mental hospital again, even at age 43. As far as dealing with the gang rape in 1994.

I have struggled with my Bi-polar Disorder since 1978, when I became 17 years old. I have been hospitalized over and over throughout my life, always on some type of medications. The drugs only made me have more frequent highs and the lows became more frequent. The rape and what happened after that had so much to do with me relapsing due to the PTSD, one thing would trigger another. I feel like my whole life, I've really struggled due to my mental illness. My family is always comparing me to someone who functions better than me.

Self-medicating: At that time, I also had an addiction to cocaine, pot, alcohol. This continued for many years. I still recently battled with an addiction to "crack" cocaine.

Longing for death: It was a gang rape that went on for hours. I did wish they had just killed me. That would have been easier. So I thought at the time and for months after.

Low self-esteem: This affects my self-esteem over and over.

Making sound decisions is hard for me, always has been, my whole life.

Self-harm: As far as what happened to me after the rape, first rehabilitation for 3 months, then sober living for about 8 months. Then I used crack cocaine again and again and again. Sexually, I became very easy. This had everything to do with the feelings I was left with by that rape.

Feeling unknown/unknowable/alone: No one truly understands my troubles except me. That's when I should become my own best friend. Unfortunately I haven't yet but I'm sure going to try.

The Turning Point

Crisis/intervention: I believe the turning point for me was going to a PTSD therapy class for 6 weeks. It was then I realized what happened to me and began to learn how not to allow myself to be triggered, or if I was what to do about it, I had tools to rely upon.

New perspective/shift in thinking: Now either you choose to hurt yourself or help yourself.

The Transformation

Increased spirituality: Myself, I was shown that my deceased husband, he has come back in the form of a blue jay.

This is the first step to now realize you can only heal if you allow the flow of God's grace to lead you on the journey ahead of you.

The trueness of their spirits will almost haunt you. Unless you are told this will happen it can be somewhat unsettling.

My experience has enhanced my level of spirituality, I connect.

God has restored me to sanity numerous times.

Forgiveness: All I know is either tap into what God is trying to tell you, which at the end of the road you will find it all comes down to forgiveness of anyone who has ever hurt you, but now the hard part, you have to be able to forgive yourself. Once you do that you become teachable.

Gratitude: For this I am truly grateful. But, am I grateful enough to truly let go and trust that God will give me all that I need, or want? That is the true question to me. Even after coming to the other side of such serious afflictions, I still at times question "Will I be taken care of by God?" Of course I will.

Painful awakening: Myself and my daughter dealing with her father's sudden death really is an issue you constantly repeat dealing with, due to the fact that it is and will always be unfinished feelings that arise. When you are truly awake to feel all the stages of this, it is a process which is very painstaking. I myself did most of it in therapy.

My Bi-polar Disorder has created me to suffer behind co-dependency issues concerning all people I come in contact with up until now (the present). I'm for the first time looking at it seriously.

I realize now that if I stay completely honest with myself, I will be able to recover from all of these maladies.

A miracle: To even feel that you can be at all worthwhile after all of this is a miracle.

New life: I have to make a new life for me first. I kept putting someone else's life first, and then I try to see where it is my turn, but my turn never happens.

Acceptance: It is a long process of acceptance.

Betrayal of trust: I do have a tendency to trust people too easily, then somehow they hurt me.

Sense of movement and breakthrough: Even after coming to the other side of such serious afflictions, I still at times question "Will I be taken care of by God?"

At the end of the road you will find it all comes down to forgiveness.

Allow the flow of God's grace to lead you on the journey ahead of you.

I've been through so many serious things and come out the other side.

This leads me down my journey in my head.

The Upperworld

New identity/survivor: Being a survivor.

My life up until now has been full of love, laughter, sorrow, disappointment of myself and my children, but somehow we survive.

Life is what you make of it. I really am a survivor.

Telling the story/sharing the trauma: Now I just wish I could go to each one of their [the rapists'] mothers and tell them what they did to me.

Self-love: I love Susannah today.

Living legacy: His [her husband's] name was John Jay. Life was waiting for him but he made a choice to give up. His

Tales of Awakening

legacy will always live on through me.

James

My second interview was with James, a 47-year-old Caucasian male with 20 years of sobriety from alcohol addiction who had gone through a severe depression following a separation from his wife and child. He was active in a 12-step program, and was willing to share his experience in order to further psychological research in the area of recovery from devastating events. He was less verbose and articulate than Susannah, yet a number of useful themes emerged in his interview as well. The 15 themes illustrated by NMUs from his interview follow.

The Underworld

Estrangement from loved one: The day she told me she wanted a separation, the worst day of my life, not because I was losing her but because I was losing my baby.

Intense pain: That was the beginning of the worst pain I had ever felt in my life. I couldn't eat, sleep, turn off my head. I couldn't stop feeling the intense pain of losing my child. This pain lasted for a month—the worst pain of my life.

Life-changing trauma: I had hoped the whole time that we would get back together so I could be with my son all the time again, then she informed me that she had found someone else, and I realized that my son wouldn't be coming back—I drove through Hidden Valley that day crying so hard that tears were squirting out of my eyes (just like on the cartoons).

Lack of eros: How I got depressed, I was in an unfulfilling relationship which was almost dead.

When we had sex for the last time, I didn't pull out soon enough, so she got pregnant.

I tried to make the best of a less than adequate situation. We were never really happy. She was frigid and never fulfilled my needs in any real, satisfying way. It was a tenuous marriage.

The Turning Point

Crisis: I started thinking that drinking alcohol might make the pain go away. Being a recovering alcoholic, I knew I was in trouble.

Intervention: I had 16 years of sobriety at this time, and I knew I had to take action soon, so I found out what time my old favorite meetings were taking place and where.

The Transformation

Telling the story/sharing trauma: First I went to the Friday night speaker meeting and saw my friend and shared my story with him. The following Monday, I went to the men's stag meeting and dropped the rock. I shared my story about how my wife left me and how I was in the worst pain of my life and how I started to think that drinking might help. I cried right there in front of everyone.

Receiving support: I received the loving support from the men in that meeting I had hoped for. The rest of the meeting was all about the men in that room sharing with me and telling me it will be okay, it just takes time. They shared their phone numbers with me and encouraged me to call.

Taking action:

Social: I did call.

Spiritual: I started going to meetings every night that I could and reading Chapter 5 out of the Big Book of Alcoholics Anonymous every day. When I was at work, instead of thinking about how I missed my family, I would think about what people in the meeting shared the night before. I would think about what I was going to share that night or what I had shared the night before.

Psychological - Blocking: I got a set of wireless headphones and listened to loud music all day at work so I wouldn't have to listen to my head.

Physical - Exercise: I also started exercising regularly as a means of dulling the pain.

The Upperworld

Continued improvement: Gradually the intense pain (the deadness) went away; it was a slow process.

Gratitude: I am grateful to the rooms of Alcoholics Anonymous for saving my life.

Sense of having returned to life: I may never have come

out of my deadness if not for AA.

Frank

My third interview was with Frank, a 33-year-old Caucasian male who works in the real estate industry. Frank spoke about issues strikingly similar to those of James, in terms of suffering through a divorce, separation from his son, and struggling with a drinking problem. Key differences were Frank's alcoholism being a present-time issue during his divorce and his grieving the loss of his wife as well as his child. Frank presented a "roller-coaster" description of being in the Upperworld first, then the Underworld, then finding his way back, whereas the other participants began their stories with their presence in the Underworld.

Frank, like the previous interviewees, expressed a poignantly deep desire to contribute his experience in order to help others who have gone or are going through severe tragedies. He stated that he did not want anyone else to feel as desperate and alone as he had during his crisis, and that it would have helped him to know then that he would survive, as he knows now. Frank's interview was quite detailed in terms of information as well as themes. The following 32 themes were identified, illustrated by their respective NMUs.

The Upperworld

Surreal bliss*:* I met the girl of my dreams. It really was love at first sight. Our attraction to each other was intense . . . both physical and emotional. And we were best of friends. Every free minute that we had we spent together. I knew early on that this would be the girl I would marry and spend the rest of my life with. I was so happy, always knowing I had someone to come home to that loved and cared for me.

I have many happy memories of us in that tiny place, building our lives together. I asked Katie to marry me. Of course she said yes, and I was overjoyed to know that we would be spending the rest of our lives together.

New life: We started our new life together as husband, wife, and son. This first year of his life was a wonderful, happy time. I remember being at work and not being able to focus on anything, just wanting to get home to see my son. My love with Katie remained strong.

The Underworld

Loss of eros: After the first year of his [their son's] life, the passionate love left, and we became more like business partners.

Estrangement: Katie started associating herself with new friends. Their influence over her was strong. Before long, my income and financial stability became an issue. We became more and more distant because of the insecurities I felt.

Loss of self-esteem: I remember how belittled I felt.

Life-altering trauma: The process server pulled divorce

papers out of his briefcase and told me Katie had filed for divorce. I was shocked. . . . I was stunned. He left me holding the papers that would change my life. I went into my manager's office hysterical.

Betrayed trust: I then knew something was horribly wrong. My wife was out of the country, and my son was nowhere to be found.

Disbelief: How could someone who said they loved me and vowed to spend the rest of their life with me do this to me? I was hoping this whole nightmare would come to an end. How could God do this to me? How could my wife do this to me?

Bargaining: I told her I was very disappointed in the way she handled this. I begged her to get together the next day and pleaded with her not to go through with this. I told her I thought this was absolutely crazy. I tried everything that I could to convince her not to go through with the divorce.

Annihilation: I used marijuana occasionally. Katie and her attorney now had the ammunition they needed to destroy me. And they did.

Intolerable pain: I became deeply depressed. I missed her dearly and missed my son beyond comprehension.

Self-medicating: I turned to something far more evil to comfort me . . . alcohol.

Whatever I could get to numb the pain.

Suicidal ideation/emotional breakdown: My de-pression

became more and more serious. There were many nights that I laid in bed contemplating my suicide. I lost my focus at work.

Withdrawal: I withdrew from my friends, my family, and life. I was in the worst physical shape that I had ever been in my life.

Anhedonia: I just didn't care about life anymore. The only joy that I ever had during this time was the time I spent with Jack [his son]. After spending a week with him and then him being away, my depression came to an all-time low.

Self-harm: I ate like a pig, drank like a fish, and was preparing myself to die. I went to a bar and sat at a table by myself and started feeling very sorry for myself. After a few hours of hard drinking, I passed out on the table.

The Turning Point

Crisis: The bartender remembered that I had been in recently with my friend Jim. He called Jim, and Jim was my knight in shining armor. He came and rescued me and took me back home. I was so intoxicated that I could not even walk on my own. He literally had to carry me to his car.

Intervention: My parents and friends came over later that night and had an intervention with me. They all begged and pleaded with me to get my health together for the sake of my son and for myself. One of my friends reminded me how painful it was for her to grow up without her father and how devastating it would

Heidi Elowitch (Taylor)

be for my son to grow up without his.

The Transformation

Becoming sober: I started the first day of my sobriety. I believe that my depression was triggered by divorce, but was intensified by alcohol. As I began to clean myself up, I began to sleep better and began to take better care of myself. I was still grossly out of shape and overweight.

Taking action:

Legal: Our divorce was final, and I was awarded a full Standard Possession order with Jack. I also became determined to turn my life around.

Physical - Diet: I cut carbs out of my diet

Physical - Exercise: I began walking/jogging an hour a night. Over the next 9 months, I lost 70 pounds and began feeling better about myself.

Spiritual: I began going to church. . . . I became closer to the Lord.

Seeking forgiveness: I asked Him for His forgiveness.

Seeking healing: I asked for Him to heal me.

Seeking wholeness: I asked for Him to make me whole again.

Social connections: I got involved with a Sunday School class which is geared toward single parents.

Awakening to universality of experience: After going a few times I realized I was not the only person in the world going through the pain that I did. Joining this class was the best thing I could have ever done at that time.

Sense of movement: Over this last year I have just started to put this painful experience behind me and move on.

The Upperworld

Sense of growth: I have grown as a parent.

Hopefulness: I look forward to my future and being able to watch Jack grow up to be a man.

Health/self-care: I am maintaining my health, diet, and work-out routine.

Gratitude: I am surrounded by the most wonderful, loving friends anyone could ever ask for.

Mary

My fourth interview was with Mary. Mary is a 41-year-old, married mother of two daughters. She is of mixed ethnic and religious background. She is a singer and a musician. Mary was very nervous about her interview, about whether her information would be "good enough" or "important enough" to contribute to a doctoral-level project and whether she would be able to tell her experience of the phenomena in the "right way." I reassured her that there was no "right" or "wrong" way to convey her life experiences, that the experience itself was of significant value to the study, and went over the informed consent in detail, making sure she understood that she should not participate if it made her feel uncomfortable or upset, and she could decline or take time to think about it and get back to me. Like the other participants, Mary stated that she felt she had truly lived the topic and would feel positive if sharing her struggles contributed to a greater good.

Mary spoke of many traumas, ranging from the death of one parent to rejection by the other, being a homeless teenager on the streets, and an unplanned pregnancy. Her story of coming to life again after many times of deadness produced material that was rich and heartbreaking and joyous. The 26 themes followed by their respective NMUs follow. Mary began with the following statement:

> Where does one begin to describe a section, sections? A part, parts? Of their own life about living in darkness and succumbing to the light? I have no idea. Is that accurate? I dunno. Well, I shall do my best. Please, Heidi, excuse my lack of verbal abilities and all that goes with that. As I do fancy myself a composer/ lyricist, I may detail too much in my talking . . . yeah, I dunno if that makes any sense. . . . I will work on keeping my answers as short and precise as possible. . . . For you to entrust me in this project I am grateful for the opportunity. . . With that said . . .

The Underworld

Sense of exclusion: Needless to say, but I will, I had an obscured sense growing up on how people really treated others. I didn't know I wasn't the "norm" but soon found out. I was born to a Scott-Irish mother and a Fijian-Pakistani father. My father was of the Islamic faith, Muslim. My mother of the Catholic faith. My life was very sheltered. My life was planned out for me:

education, career, marriage—YES— marriage.

Loss of loved one: Continuing on to age 12. . . . Father, whom I love, respect, relate to, and adore, died a very unexpected death. The pain ate at me.

Rejection: Mother, who never spoke to me, and scared me, and drank alcohol, and ate pork, was now all I have. I never saw my parents give affection to one another. It is the Muslim custom for man and wife not to sleep in the same room. My mother did not like me. I was terrified of her.

Multiple traumas: Continuing on to age 19. After years of turmoil—juvenile hall, getting kicked out of home, cutting, starving, bulimia, rape, homeless, born again Christian group home—I found myself pregnant.

Lost opportunities: I had lost out on so much in life. Having had been an honor student somewhere in time and had scholarship opportunities, a once-in-a-lifetime audition I never showed up to (I was locked up), to Julliard. . . . Here I was, pregnant. Fuck. Yep. That was it. I fucked up . . . again.

Emotional deadness: Now out of school and depressed all the time . . . no one pushing me to do or be anything. It was like I didn't exist. I did what I had to do. I kept my baby. I wasn't going to be my mother. A stranger. A drunk. Mean and abusive. Alone. I was living solely for this little soul which was now growing inside of my starved little body.

Move on to about a year later, my darling baby now about

Heidi Elowitch (Taylor)

2 years old. I found myself homeless after messing up a friendship with a girl I was staying with, a young mother herself, because of my baby's father. I remember being so tired. Hunger for me was not an option. I ate whatever I could to survive. I was nursing my baby. I had to make sure she was always safe and fed. It was the most difficult time in my life. All of the people who said they were my friends no longer cared. I was scared and alone. I had a cloth baby carrier I tied to my chest. I held that baby close to me all of the time. I remember walk-walk-walking like I had someplace to go. I didn't panhandle. I knew from a previous homeless life that someone would notice my baby and take her. I was terrified to ask anyone for help and those I did ask turned a blind eye to my existence. What seemed an eternity was really only a few months' time.

Abusive relationships: My baby's father came back into the picture again. I had no one else . . . so I agreed to move with him to Washington. We lived—my baby and I—in Washington for almost exactly 2 years. I was abused by my baby's father. It started when I was pregnant. He dragged me by the hair once when I went following him to the corner where he bought his crack. The crack dealer just stood there laughing and howling at me while the boy kicked me and punched me. I was always getting into trouble looking for that boy. Once I had to leave my baby with strangers, punk rock kids I had just met, so I could find that boy. He left with my last five dollars to buy formula (I had to stop nursing 'cause I was sick) and didn't come back. I waited almost 2 days.

Self-doubt: While wandering around L.A. looking for him, I came across some guys with masks . . . it was Halloween . . . who acted like they knew me . . . said my guy was coming right back . . . what a fool I was . . . I didn't listen to my intuition . . . I got mugged. . . . What a dummy. . . . I digress. . . . Finally he left for good. He went on a binge and took all my savings. The entire lot of it, $300. That was it, all I had. Once again I was screwed...fucked.

The Turning Point

An opportunity: My mother had a change of heart and sent me a bus ticket back home and back into her life. I jumped at the chance. Back home things started to brighten up a little. I was very blessed and lucky to have begged and pleaded my way back home to my mother's again . . . get back on welfare. I lived with her in silence. . . She believed me to be an abomination and would not look at me or speak to me. I paid rent . . . cleaned . . . stayed to myself.

An identity shift: I was changed though. I was humbled from the responsibility of motherhood. I knew I was going to keep my promise and always be true to me and my baby. Everything else didn't matter. However I was still young and naïve, vulnerable and stupid. I did what I thought I had to do . . . so I got on welfare. I believed I was less than any and every person. I believed I was dumb and a loser.

The Transformation

A crisis: She sold the house. I was now 23. I moved to Venice.

An awakening: I joined a popular and hard-working rock band. I found out that people enjoyed me entertaining them. It was a tremendous time in my life. I was awakening to my potential I had lost somewhere along the way. Still a lot of growth was to be had. A lot of knowledge to be gained. I experienced many hard and difficult times again. Nothing like what I had already gone through.

The Upperworld

A new life:

A teacher: I was able to teach my daughter how to read and write and play musical instruments before she began kindergarten. She is an amazing woman now and about ready to graduate from college soon and continue her amazing experiences.

A successful parent: I am a loved and proud and blessed mama.

A thriving career: My music is now listened to around the world.

A good relationship: I have met and married my best friend. We have a beautiful 5-year-old daughter together.

Stable housing: I am a homeowner.

Tales of Awakening

Wisdom: I have learned a great deal from my experiences. There are people who, if given the chance, will hurt you for their own benefits. There are people in our lives to teach us, whether it be positive or negative.

Gratitude: Each experience is worth it. What we take from it is up to us. I am grateful for that knowledge. It has saved me to know this. Anger will turn a person sour.

Forgiveness: To forgive is the greatest gift one can give or receive.

The boy and I keep in contact. He has repeated "our" scenario now with a few other girls that have no idea of self-love and what that is. He has continued on his path of sadness and destruction, and sometimes he's okay.

My mom and I have also healed, for the most part. I love her and would do anything for my mom.

Experiences were destined: I have had extreme experiences. Lots of death. More than anyone should have to go through. . . . But . . . I guess I had to.

Self-discovery: I have—and am—discovered myself through living.

Healing: I have healed myself through time.

Blessed: I have been truly blessed with knowing we are the creators of our own destinies. You are what you think you are.

Empowerment: I am master of my destiny… and I fuckin' love it!

Hope: I am full of hope for a better world…for everyone…I know what got me to where I am has and always will be hope. I never stopped dreaming for happiness. I got it. That's all I ever wanted. That's all I ever needed. It is constant.

Wholeness: I am whole, and I'm okay.

Holly

Holly is a 39-year-old Caucasian female. She is a divorced mother of a son and daughter, both in their late teens. She works as·an emergency room nurse in a small city. Holly, much like Mary, has had a life so filled with catastrophe and tragedy it is nearly incomprehensible to believe it has all happened to one individual in one lifetime. Holly was very motivated to share her journey with the interviewer. She expressed the desire of several of the participants to assist the investigator in producing something which may be of value for those experiencing emotional deadness, and for those trying to support them.

Holly had spent several years journaling and blogging about her various life experiences and is a gifted artist, writer, and photographer. Her interview was richly detailed and her language poetic and engaging. Holly's background and expressive language skills enabled her to provide a very detailed interview with an abundance of themes. She spoke of many issues: her own struggles with illness as well as her loved ones illnesses and death; divorce; bereavement; and depression as an entity unto itself. Holly's interview yielded 60 themes. The themes from her interview follow, accompanied by their respective NMUs.

The Underworld

Emotional deadness: Kinesthetic properties:

Dark: There were days when, in spite of the weather, when the sun did not   shine in my life or in my heart.

It was difficult to see the sunshine from the bottom of that well, because it was a dark, demoralizing, and heavy place.

I often found I shined so brightly but burned out much too quickly!

Empty: Sometimes, my emotional resources appeared to have disappeared.

Dry: For me, the well was dry.

Low: I believe I was at the bottom, both emotionally and physically.

Stuck/hopeless: I also believed I would always feel that way.

It felt as though my life was on hold.

I was just waiting.

Weighty: It was difficult to see the sunshine from the bottom of that well because it was a dark, demoralizing, and heavy place.

It was difficult to pull myself up, emotionally, when my body was not healthy, but it could and had to be done.

For me, there were warning signs. I was more lethargic than usual. Occasionally it was a medication, which was a real

Heidi Elowitch (Taylor)

downer for me.

I'd been walking around feeling like there's a big weight hanging over me ready to fall at any moment.

Draining: Getting things done was a chore. Making plans beyond the next day took all of my willpower.

Painful: Pain is hell . . . most of the day what I felt was a physical pain. The best I can describe it is to liken it to when your foot falls asleep. Imagine that feeling in your chest. Then when you move your foot to wake it up—the shooting pain you feel. Imagine that feeling in your chest all day long. That's what it felt like.

Helpless: But I couldn't shake it. I couldn't do anything to make it go   away. I just ached for him [referring to a close friend, Joe, who had died].

Incessant: There was no relief.

Foreign: Depression was just there, like the unwelcome, unplanned for guest who arrived at the door.

Loss of former abilities: Sometimes the cause of my depression was some event which had triggered a painful reminder of something I could no longer do.

Brutally real: I think I would worry about someone who, when faced with daily pain and limitations, took the attitude "Oh well, la-de-da, life is just a bowl of cherries." Sometimes it's the pits. It's not exactly what we had planned for our lives. Acceptance of such painful facts and pain-filled lives can, quite frankly, be a bitch.

To me, it is simply a fact of life, at least the kind of life I have to lead.

Self-doubt/blame: For me, there was usually a cause, such as pushing myself beyond my physical limits. Guess I'm just not too bright. It's either that or I am just too ornery and stubborn to accept this fix my body is in. I don't customarily wise up until I am exhausted or in extreme pain or both.

Emotional lability: Mary Poppins meets Dracula. Yes, I think that pretty well sums it up.

Some days my emotions had a range which was both surprising, alarming, and confusing. Within a 24-hour period, I often experienced both laughter and tears. Many of us who have chronic illness accompanied by daily pain experience the highs and lows. I would even go so far as to say all of us are . . . at one time or another . . . depression can visit at any moment . . . is that any surprise? I think that's a normal enough reaction, don't you?

I think I had experienced more emotions and feelings in those few weeks than in any week since facing my own illnesses in my journey.

I saw Joe that morning [before he died]. I think even the street traffic below stopped and the earth fell totally silent, with the exception of the crickets, apparently. Emotions coulda carried the fucking world cross-country.

I will tell you our doctor had been my crying sponge, he'd

Heidi Elowitch (Taylor)

wiped away kabillions of tears, yet that morning he cried with me.

Joe told me to continue my soulshining love. I was saddened beyond belief.

I have had many, many times of what I call "Spontaneous Crying." It happens so often. Here I am. (Cries).

One thing is for sure . . . fear tries hard to be the boss.

Hope is everything, isn't it? It's anticipation, desire, and the expectation for the best to come.

So, I am going forward with my life as if I was the luckiest person on earth. I may cry for no apparent reason. Many factors can cause me to flip that emotional switch, such as the turn for the worst of America and the hardships we face, old memories or insensitive behavior by someone else, often, however, the reasons for depression and unstable emotions are not actually based on any direct cause. Those are the days when I am not a reasonable human being.

Losing a loved one: And oddly enough, the one thing I thought I was prepared for brought me to my knees. . . . Joe's cancer taking him like a swift river in the dead of winter.

Cancer took someone so, so close to me . . . like the sun takes a snowman . . . if it freezes, the snowman does not melt, stays the same, yet will never get bigger. If it gets warmer a bit, the snowman melts a bit; on a hot sunny day, the snowman melts a lot. In his last few days, Joe's cancer was taking him and one day the sun claimed its share.

Tales of Awakening

Anticipatory grief: A feeling of loss before a death or dreaded event occurs is an unsettling, emotional time for me. I'll have to deal with my own feelings of vulnerability and mortality, as well as the stresses of helping a friend cope through dying. You'd think after my life experiences and working as a nurse I'd have the courage to say "I'm having an anticipatory grief day."

I hope you'll learn from my experience and tell people you're going through anticipatory grief.

I grieve because I care. Anticipatory grief shapes my life, helps me define who I am, and who I'm meant to be. And when pain comes, I'm offered drugs. Instead of offering hugs and support, we're offered denial.

Time of transition: It's a powerful time of transition that brought Joe and I even closer.

It's amazing how the two tiny words "any day" spoken by a doctor can create a sense of urgency in those close to the one whom those words are spoken. In a very powerful way, also, those words bring a certain freedom, they provide permission to step away from the responsibilities of daily life and attend to the profound and transformative issues that arise around the ending of a life.

When I step back from all that is happening and get a bit of perspective, I really do see the blessing of this time. It is so easy to place life on hold, to wait for some momentous—or not so momentous—event in order to move on. I have seen it in myself and in my career as a nurse. I'm faced with life and death constantly. We wait for the helicopter to land, the ambulance transporting someone critical or severely injured, we wait for a phone call, we wait for any small or big news, we worry continuously, nerves and emotions are alive and full of anxiety.

Desperation: Please, I implored people, even if you were a complete stranger, or a lurker, please in the spirit of passion, reach out, please, I beg you, pray, pray and plead for my Joe!

I found my mind running in all directions, looking for help, trying to ease the pain I was feeling, and everyone else who felt it, and I wanted to be there for them but I felt the deep pain of feeling helpless, of not understanding.

For a couple years, the voices inside my head repeatedly shouted . . . shield me from the world. Numb me inside . . . make me feel no emotions. I'd soak my pillow in tears.

Survivor guilt: I had my bout with cancer in 1999. I am one of the lucky ones. I have been granted hundreds of "one more days."

We fought the same disease, in different ways, yes. But hoping for the same outcome. . . . My prayer for Joe: "Go forth in peace, for you have followed the good road. Go forth without fear, for He that created you has sanctified you, has always protected you, and loves you."

I love Joe, much more than you can possibly know.

Many, many questions arise in my mind when someone

close to me is seriously ill. It takes a while to realize that these questions do not have one answer. They have many answers, appear in different ways, and may have different impacts on me at different times. In a sense, a finger is being pointed in my direction. These questions are demanding a response. I cannot be free from answering. Life itself is demanding a reply.

Sense of failure: It blows my mind sometimes to think that I seemed so weak and helpless at times.

There are times when I can't rid myself of the burdens, pains, struggles. Why does that seem so difficult at times?

The last few weeks were stressful for me, as Joe was coming to the last of his days and a lot of disrespect had occurred to me on a website that I was active on. Neither happenings were exactly unexpected, but both were jarring. And while the warm smiles and warmer hugs from my son had helped ease the pain, I noticed something else happening underneath. Something in the eyes as we looked at each other, a kind of knowing, as if the sum of our secrets, our successes and failures, our hopes and fears, would never add up to a life complete. By what measure do we examine our existence? Should we even try as hard as we do?

As I think about the lives of the ones I've already lost (my brother's death anniversary is coming up). I think and wonder about the treasures they discovered in life. I wonder if they'd found them all. Does anybody, ever?

And suddenly, self-doubt came crawling in, leaving a trail

of pockmarks and scars in its wake. Two pathways spread out in front of me, both darkened by the shadow of the future. Which, in its own way, was exciting, but also incredibly unnerving. I'd always considered myself a dreamer—am proud of this, too—and have spent a lot of energy exploring both pathways. To choose one over another was perhaps the most horrifying decision I ever had to make.

Desire/need for escape: I seemed to get lost in other people's lives. The funny thing is I loved to get lost in other people's lives.

I was so frightened of my reality and exhausted from my emotional pain that I too often tried to alter my reality. Which only made things worse.

Sense of being "stuck": Another day . . . I waited. . . How often did I put my life on hold waiting for some external circumstance to resolve itself? For that is all I could do.

Bereavement grief: My best friend Joe passed away. I know . . . but . . . but nothing . . . words cannot even explain. I treasure the memories that I have of us together. Death is so permanent for those who haven't tried it. Death is too tragic when destiny shows up early. Death is anything and everything.

That which does not kill you makes you stronger—who ever said that? How is that possible? Clearly it's not a reference to physical damage. Rarely do fatal injuries ever result in making another person any physically stronger. So how is it that emotional damage that is so great that it crushes my very soul can eventually make me a stronger, better person?

It seems at best illogical and at worst, incredibly self-centered, that one should view a horrible event in a way that ultimately will be of benefit to you. In my experience, people that have undergone excruciatingly difficult emotional challenges have come out of them variously scared, sometimes angry, bitter, and ultimately scarred in ways even they don't comprehend.

Whatever setback or disappointment or failure I encountered—once upon a time it didn't matter because I knew I could call Joe, drive my fast car to his house at any hour, and collapse into him. And he'd tell me that I'm strong and brave, and the words of his friendship healed my broken hurts, my anger, my feelings, no matter what it was about. Together we could do and be anything—that's a true friendship. Now, I feel like nothing. It's so wrong without him. My strength and security is weaker without Joe.

On the anniversary death of my little brother, James, he passed away in 2003, I sat alone and had emotions on top of emotions. I also had Joe in my thoughts and James inside my heart. Though hundreds of people walked past my brother every day, James was one of the few who stopped to talk. My brother greeted the homeless people in his area by name, sometimes bringing them coffee, lunches, and on a few occasions that I know of, inviting homeless people into his house to play pool with him.

Heidi Elowitch (Taylor)

He loved this world so much and wanted so badly to succeed in it, to have what most of us take for granted—a good job, a healthy body, and most importantly, someone to love. Lost . . .

Leaving so many others behind . . . but I always think . . . and find it funny how I'm the one left behind.

I know it's Joe who is gone, but so much of me left with him. I've lost parts of me that I never expect to see again. Will I be whole again? My thoughts, my actions, my words, my face— I've changed. I don't know who I see when I look at myself—it's surely not me. It can't be me who looks so broken and tired and sad. It can't be me who feels so much fear all the time. I've been preparing myself for Joe's death since 2006—telling myself all through each day that it's going to be okay, it's going to be alright—but I didn't believe it. I was talking to an old friend on the phone today. When he asked me how I was doing, I said, "Okay." He told me my voice changed when I said it. I didn't say this to him but my voice changed because I was lying. I'm not okay.

Sense of being less fortunate: It seemed my friends were nowhere to be found. I made a game out of measuring my losses against their victories. One of my friends buys a house, my car shits on me; I have two kids, no child support, I'm busting my butt, life bounces; another gets married, people are taking vacations, I was getting ready to leave the man I love-d (voice breaks). I was bitter.

Sense of emptiness: The tears went away, and I was left with this incredible emptiness.

Sense of being attacked by god: It seemed to me as if everything in my life was being destroyed. The early start of summer, in 2004, I started having symptoms. 2003 was the darkest I'd ever faced, my brother died and my health tumbled. I was certain someone up there hated me.

The Turning Point

A shift in awareness: I latched onto the Serenity Prayer—"God grant me the serenity to accept the things I cannot change, the courage to change the things I can, and the wisdom to know the difference"—but I misunderstood its true meaning. I focused on the first line and believed that I should accept this new existence; essentially, that if my life was to be one big thunder storm of misery, then I should just resign myself to my fate. In other words, that prayer became a way for me to justify my right to continue to feel sad and lost for myself.

Awakening: In the middle of 2006 was around the time I was busy shaking my fist at the gods that I started noticing a few ordinary occurrences were bringing some levity to my doleful existence. The sun came out. The snow melted. The flowers and trees in my favorite park began to bloom. I became aware of these things, whereas before I doubt I would have noticed anything above my shoe-line. I saw that time was passing and my pain was subsiding. At some point, I realized that what I really needed to do was focus on the second line of the prayer instead of the first.

Action: I needed to find the courage to change the things that I could. In this case, that meant my reactions to the events that confronted me. Instead, I started to spend even more time with my son, and I read some good books, and got back to thinking about my book and spending more time writing in my journal. I started to have a better understanding and appreciation for the human condition, with all its attendant weaknesses.

Appreciation: I realized that I had all the things that my brother sought—a good career, a stable mind, and most importantly, I woke up every morning in the presence of someone whom I loved more than anything else in the world, someone who was struggling along with me, and yet his love never wavered, never faltered. Even when life turned dark, my son was there.

Gratitude: I looked back on the past years and remember James was always there for me and my kids; he was ready with a Kleenex, the thousands of hugs I took for granted, the special fleece he wore because he said it would absorb the most tears, the cups of coffee that magically appeared at the most opportune moments, his despondency rather than resentment, when I'd get pissed at him—if you're wondering, yes, I did tell James when he snubbed up, he needed advice, influence, and a chick to tell him to smarten his ass up—these things made me love him more.

Wisdom: Am I a stronger, better person because my

brother died? No, unequivocally I am not. Did I learn something having lived through this ordeal? Yes. That difficult time had a ripple effect on every other relationship in my life but, most importantly, my relationship with myself. I examined and dissected everything in my life, looking for understanding. In the process, some things fell away. Those that didn't will endure. From destruction comes regrowth. In that sense, I suppose that which didn't kill me did make me stronger. Perhaps . . . this is all just dumb . . . (laughing a little). I can be such a cry-baby!! (Cries). I should just suck it up and hold myself together. Perhaps when I'm depressed . . . I need help . . . or maybe I'm just goin' crazy!!!

Letting go: I finally threw away two potted plants that I brought home after the funeral. I had tried to nurse them back, but they were pitifully ugly, and it was rather depressing. One was a Peace Lily. My little Ms. Lily—my Siamese cat—kept chewing it up and it looked like hell. I don't have a green thumb.

The Transformation

Reaching out/getting advice: So one day I asked my colleague, I need someone who can inspire me, same time by being practical. I don't want to listen to all that highly motivated stuff. Something that someone doesn't need to tell or explain. It could be anyone, anything. Yes, even a non-living cup that could tell me—"Have a cup of tea before it gets cold." For me it would be like saying, a blind man trying to access the web. And I heard the most inspiring words within 5 seconds after I asked my colleague. Fast he was. He said—"Listen Holly . . . life has been crude to you for a while. . . . Go explore, find out, don't restrict yourself . . . just because you are lacking resources and energy." I felt I got the answer. See. Answers always lie within the inner core of our souls; sometimes we need inspirations from others. After all, questions come from there only.

My colleague said, "Holly, our bodies have the knowledge and the heart has the wisdom—far beyond the seeing of the eyes, the listening of the ears, the sensing touch of our hands, and even the sniffing of our smart noses. Indeed, listening with our bodies is a supremely receptive experience, for the body is a totally sensing instrument." How true, I thought.

Open to healing: That's my inspiration to feel the healing in "my" days. Others around me inspire me and share their healing inspirations. Inspiration not only makes the work easy and good but also improves the relationships we have. Who would like to be in the company of a demotivating person? Inspire, inspire, indeed.

Discouragement: In the ups and downs of life, one day or another day, how many times did I feel that there was kind of a dissatisfaction in life? No satisfaction in self-work that I was pursuing; in my personal life, I was getting dull day by day; and friends were far away. So much to achieve and no way was leading to there. So many hazards, uncertainty.

Tales of Awakening

Was it feasible, or was I being non-practical? All these thoughts clouded over.

The numinous: There was this arousal of my mind to special unusual activity or creativity . . . some action or power of moving my intellect or emotions.

Hope: Then a plain thought of hope lightened up the dark roads.

Facing fear: I wanted to learn how to stop running, even for a little while. I had so much fear about looking at illness and loss. I feared that if I faced Joe's suffering, it would make me feel helpless. Actually, the opposite was true, on my good strong days. In this way, I become alive and strong, reclaiming for myself the fullness of all my experiences. I thought, when I learn how to master this, I may even discover that the pain comes holding a gift in my hands. I knew there were no answers. And I knew I'm not alone. I wanted so badly to be strong and positive. But, I didn't have it. Not yet, anyway. I was searching. I felt I would find it. Right then, though, I was terrified.

Insight: I could see that the only true comfort would come from understanding; the only real healing would come from the truth. If I learned to listen closely, I would find that the pain itself had a meaning. It was there to be listened to.

Faith: One week, I kept telling myself that everything would be okay. One day, I'll know the reason for this and it will all make sense. I kept telling myself that I'm going to do something good with this pain. I'm going to surprise myself. I do try to appreciate the blessings. I had the most amazingly beautiful friendship with Joe. I have a beautiful life—that not even death can take away from me.

If I'm going to live with physical and emotional pain; however, the only way to come to a peace about it was to let my spiritual beliefs use it in my life in any way that seems fit. I rested and waited for the purpose to be revealed. Each of us can find a purpose in the pain. Pain is undeniable.

For me it has taken a combination of medical treatment therapy and faith, plus plain old hard work!

Making a decision: An old friend of Joe's (and a friend of mine, too) talked to me quite some time ago. It was with her that I recounted all the blessings Joe and I had. At the same time, I expressed my hatred for Joe's primary care physician. It was then that I realized I might have to make a decision. Do I continue to loathe and condemn him for not finding the cancer sooner? The signs were definitely there and he neglected to act upon his findings. I was so infuriated. He could have started chemo and radiation, then there were discussions back in October about a liver transplant, which never transpired, 'cause Joe's PCP [primary care physician] waited too long to refer him to a specialist. On the other hand, it would have been more time he spent sick and scared. Or, do I thank God, whom I've hated for so many months, that the people who love Joe had to watch cancer ravage him?

Navigating the unknown: I consider myself a fairly logical, rational person. If I have a question or problem, I can generally figure out where to find the answer or solution. Before the internet, this meant looking things up in books, encyclopedias, dictionaries, asking doctors, therapists . . . but, I couldn't find a tutorial on grief. There was no "how-to" or Frequently Asked Questions to help me get through what I was feeling. How was I supposed to work when I periodically broke down crying? How was I supposed to get through the day when the first thing I did when I woke up was think of my best friend Joe and my brother? I knew there were no easy answers. And I knew I was not alone.

The Upperworld

Hindsight: Now I've learned that it's easy to say "I struggled," but it is infinitely harder to live it in the present tense. It's easy to say "time heals" but excruciatingly difficult to wait out the sentence of grief.

Life has had its challenges, but it also has its gifts.

Illness, death, and losses in life are only part of what has been taken away. Some valued parts of my life, yes, but the hole is not empty. I am strong.

Confidence: I can cross all the hurdles, because I am confident.

Sense of connection: Our society is built upon the premise

that you put others down and build up yourself. Jesus tells us to put ourselves last and build up others with encouragement and love. By using my pain, I will begin to focus on others, and the pain will become more of a tool and less of a thorn. I needed personal connection for dealing with my emotional grief and my health issues. It is so comforting to read of others who have struggled with many of the same issues I have. I tell you this to offer my ear and shoulder to others when they struggle with similar issues.

Friendship is perhaps the best gift I've received in life.

I believe a good friend can be the best counsel, if I can be honest and forthright with them.

Normalizing: I know that there have been so many times when I just want to be the world's version of "normal" but here I am—the "un-normal" and I still find love and support without the pressure to overdo. I only have to get used to the idea that my thoughts, feelings, and emotions are safe with who I'm talking to, and they're also comfortable.

Paying it forward/being of service/carrying the message: It's hard to hear people respond to my grief, and in some ways, it's easier to talk about things.

We will all suffer in this world. We have each been given the opportunity to become a "wounded healer" and reach out to others who are in pain, who feel alone, isolated, depressed, abandoned.

[Near the end of her interview, Holly made the following request.]

Holly: "May I share with you, briefly, what I do for and about depression in the hope that something I have discovered might be of help to others?"

Researcher: "That would be great."

[The interview continued and the following additional themes were gleaned from that data.]

Emotional outlet: I committed myself to emotional cleansing . . . a fact I'll keep on trumpeting: healing negativity prevents toxic build up in my emotional energy field. Consistently chipping away at the negative makes more room for light in my being.

Self-awareness is my greatest ally against emotional fear and its bullying cohorts. When these brutes appear, it allows me to say, "I know you. Now scram!" Psychotherapy, introspection, meditation, journaling, and/or talking with friends all further healing. As negativity remits, my emotional energy becomes more alluring, and positive connections will gravitate to me.

Keeping a journal is just one therapy I highly recommend for grieving people.

Although every person mourns differently, journaling allows me to see how I am progressing.

Writing is a great catharsis for any problem, but especially with grief.

Patience: Hold on and wait it out. The chances are that you and I will feel better, if not today, then tomorrow. There are good days. There are bad days. The cycle will come to your rescue if you will just have faith in that and wait.

Activity/engagement/involvement: Keep busy. Do something. If you just lie there and think about how awful you feel, then you will. Act. Move. Achieve. It may only be taking a walk. Planting flowers. Writing down how you feel in a journal. Pick up a book and get lost in someone else's life. Call a friend, cry on their shoulder, then listen to what's going on in their life. Bake a batch of cookies and share them.

Hygiene: Take a hot shower or bath with tons of fragrant bubbles. Get clean. Get out of the stinky old sweatpants.

Education/self-awareness: Take a good look at your disease. Get to know your medications. Read up on them. One of them may be triggering your "lows." Do all that you can to feel at your maximum. I know that seems obvious, but we still don't do it.

Get to know your own mind, your spirit, and your disease to fight the fight that we must win to make the most of the life we have been given. Hang in there.

Exercise: Get your endorphins rolling by strolling around the neighborhood or just around your house. I lift a six pound weight. Big deal, I know, but it is something constructive for my body and my brain.

Tales of Awakening

Don't self-pity: Reach out to the experience of others. Remind yourself you are not the only person who has suffered. There are, for instance, young soldiers coming home who are coping with horrendous challenges right now, as I speak. Think of them. Say a prayer for them. If you don't pray, then send them some of your pity, your strength, and your thoughts. Don't spend it all on yourself. It will only make you more miserable.

Body language: Act "as if." Stand up as straight as you can, no slouching body language allowed. Go out in public with a smile on your face. Look as good as you can; you'll feel better, truly.

Distract: Don't feed those dismal, "poor me" thoughts. Put them aside even if it means you have to distract yourself with activity, the TV, computer, or music. Don't dwell on the downward side of this dilemma.

Play: Don't be afraid to act silly. It feels wonderful. I play with one of my critters or visit my young nieces. They don't understand depression due to their innocence. Embrace that freshness for life exuded by children and animals.

Get help: Choose your help wisely. Find some professional who knows how to help those who deal with chronic pain and illness. Ask around and if you go to someone and don't feel that "click" with them, find someone else. I still believe a good friend can sometimes be the best counsel if you can be honest and forthright with them.

Heidi Elowitch (Taylor)

Tell your story: Everybody has a story, and because we all do, when we hear each other's stories, we feel suddenly connected. Stories are the great river that runs through the human landscape, and our individual stories are the little creeks that flow through us all to join the river at its source.

When I tell my story, I open myself to the level of fragility, which, as human beings, we all share, for no matter how different our stories, at the bottom of them all is the well of pain from which we have each sipped a draft.

To tell and share our stories to ourselves first, we can then try to make some sense of it.

I told my story on paper 233 times in 14 different ways . . . then on the net . . . to a friend, and it then started helping me.

Getting to the deliverance point of sharing isn't easy. To arrive at the place of the "Ahhaa!! I've made it out of the pit of hell" . . . I needed to be willing to crawl on all fours to get to the destination. This meant getting there takes courage and a lot of practice and sheer force of will. It's worth it! I started slowly by telling myself that there is such a place—a real destination, then I did whatever it took, no matter what hurdles I had to jump or walls I had to walk through, until I arrived *barefoot* to the deliverance point of acceptance of my emotional grief in managing my unsteady feelings and even my life with chronic illness.

It has helped me realize that each day is a gift. Maybe through it, I can make a difference in the life of someone else.

Tales of Awakening

Summary of Findings

In this study, the lived experience of coming to life again after a period of emotional deadness was explored by interviewing five participants (two men and three women, ages 33 to 47) about their experiences and reporting on them and by including this researcher's lived experience of the phenomenon in a separate chapter. The participants came from a range of different backgrounds, occupations, lifestyles, and belief systems.

Some of the participants had experienced the same type of traumatic events as part of their Underworld journey (e.g., rape, divorce, substance abuse, separation from a child), and others had individual experiences such as being a homeless teenage parent or enduring a painful chronic illness. Their turning points were all unique to their own lives. Meeting a new person, hearing the "right" words at the "right" time, being offered a particular opportunity, realizing they could lose something they held dear— whatever it was, each participant had an identifiable moment when they could recall changing direction to head back toward the Upperworld. As was the case for the Underworld, the participants' experiences in their stages of Transformation and the Upperworld revealed common themes (wisdom, courage) as well as individual ones (play, feeling blessed).

Eight common themes emerged from all of the interviews, which were confirmed by the participants. These major themes are, by category:

Heidi Elowitch (Taylor)

The Underworld:

    1. Major Trauma

    2. Emotional Deadness

The Turning Point:

    3. A Crisis

    4. An Intervention

The Transformation:

    5. Painful Awakening

    6. Taking Action

The Upperworld:

    7. Telling The Story/Sharing The Trauma

    8. New Life/New Identity

In addition to these common themes, several common elements were mentioned by many or most of the participants. Most of the participants described their time in the Underworld in some detail (see Table E1), mentioning feelings of complete emptiness, extreme terror, and unbearable suffering as well as feeling unknown, alone, estranged, rejected, excluded, withdrawn, anhedonic, annihilated, and emotionally broken down. They spoke of being filled with self-doubt and self-blame, being abused in numerous ways, experiencing a loss of Eros, having lowered self-esteem, and engaging in self-injurious behavior. They recalled lost opportunities, stunned disbelief, desperate bargaining, and utter hopelessness. They described various encounters of great pain, tragic losses and separations, times of isolation and exclusion, betrayals of all types, thoughts of suicide or death, and emotional deadness. The participants elaborated on their coping mechanisms, which were useful at the time but ultimately self-destructive, the two main ones being self-deprecation and self-medicating/substance abuse.

The Turning Point phase was often associated with a catastrophe followed by a shift in perspective (see Table F1). This was frequently in the form of an opportunity potentiated by another person, through either words or actions which affected the participant deeply.

The Transformation phase (see Table G1) was marked by descriptions of newfound or greater spiritual connections, painful awakening to what one had been dealing with, a sense of movement and breakthrough to a new dimension, sharing the trauma and telling the story to others, receiving support in return, and a sense of healing. Participants described taking action on multiple levels: social, legal, physical, dietary, educational, cognitive, medical, psychological, and emotional. Feelings that were shared by several of the participants include acceptance, forgiveness, gratitude, and wholeness.

The Upperworld phase (see Table H1) was described by informants as a place where they felt blessed, empowered, hopeful, blissful, grateful, forgiving, and wise. They experienced it as a time of growth, self-discovery, and destiny. Many continued to share their experience of recovery with the feeling that their

Heidi Elowitch (Taylor)

own suffering made sense if it could be used to help others and ease their suffering or give them guidance and hope.

As one might expect, certain individual themes appeared in each of the phases as well. Although it is possible that the other participants also experienced these elements, they did not articulate them specifically in their interviews. Though they did not appear as key or common themes, they were vividly and potently described by the informants who mentioned them and offer added detail to the understanding of the landscape of the Heroic journey (see Table I1). One informant offered picturesque adjectives referring to her Underworld as *weighty, dark, dry, low,* and *too real* to escape from in fantasy. Two informants identified the person who assisted in their Turning Point intervention as their "Knight in Shining Armor." One participant aptly described her Transformation stage as an "Awakening to Universal Experience." Individual elements arising in the Upperworld phase included being a survivor, a living legacy for a loved one who had died, and experiencing self-love for the first time.

The essential or common themes, derived from reviewing the individual themes, are discussed in detail in the following chapter. From these themes, a structural description of the experience of coming to life again after a period of emotional deadness is developed.

CHAPTER 5
DISCUSSION OF THE COMMON THEMES

Overview

As discussed in Chapter 4, the interviews with the six participants in this study along with this researcher's heuristic experience yielded eight common themes. These shared themes, reflecting the participants' experience of *coming to life again after a period of emotional deadness* are: (1) Major Trauma, (2) Emotional Deadness, (3) A Crisis, (4) An Intervention, (5) Painful Awakening, (6) Taking Action, (7) Sharing the Trauma/Telling the Story, and (8) New Life/New Identity.

This chapter examines each of these common themes in detail, as well as commenting on other common elements and less frequently mentioned themes contained in the individual interviews and the heuristic component. From these themes, a structural description of the experience of coming to life again after a period of emotional deadness is presented. A poststructural discussion follows.

Whereas the purpose of this study was to explore and document the lived experience of coming to life again after a period of emotional deadness, certain things became apparent to this researcher that were of interest. There were striking similarities between many of the participants' own descriptions of their journeys from the Underworld to the Upperworld and the myths and fairy tales discussed in the Literature Review. From this perspective, the participant's stories can be viewed as modern-day versions of our archetypal myths and fairy tales on the topic of the Return. The participant as the central figure in each interview or autobiographical heuristic data collection can be likened to the archetypal/mythological figures of Persephone, Inanna, the Wounded Healer, Christ, the Phoenix, Job, or one of the many characters who endures some form of intense suffering, undergoes a radical change precipitated by a crisis of some sort, often is affected or assisted in some way by a meeting with a powerful or magical being, and is reborn or resurrected in some fashion with newfound abilities or characteristics which were not present before the metamorphosis.

Additionally, it became clear to this researcher that the interviews contained some very important "do's and don'ts" for anyone—from friend, relative, significant other, or acquaintance, all the way to doctor or psychotherapist—on how to offer help or comfort and how not to harm or offend an individual undergoing the difficult process of making his or her way through the Heroic Journey. The participants all very clearly stated what things had been of value to them and which things had been experienced as hurtful or unsupportive, and delineated that they had minimal or no resources that met their direct need to understand what was happening to them when they were in the journey or to offer hope that a return was possible.

All the participants expressed their poignant desire for

Tales of Awakening

their adversity not to have been for naught and believed that, if nothing else, they could use their misfortune to benefit others undergoing the same battle in order to offer hope that survival was possible. They all communicated that it would have been of tremendous importance to them if they had had such a guide available to them in order to keep up hope and to be cognizant that they would someday be back amongst the living.

The particular features that someone experiencing an Underworld odyssey might find useful in terms of feeling understood and assured of an eventual homecoming and that might actually help in an attempt to set such a rebound in motion are summarized for the reader in Table J1. These may be beneficial to those ailing from emotional deadness as well as those attempting to understand, assist, or treat such persons, including therapists.

The Common Themes

The eight common themes which emerged from this research on the lived experience of coming to life again after a period of emotional deadness are defined here, examined in detail for each participant, and summarized from an in-depth perspective.

The Underworld

Major Trauma

The American Heritage Dictionary of the English

Language defines *trauma* as:

> "a) A wound, especially one produced by sudden physical injury; b) an emotional shock that creates substantial and lasting damage to the psychological development of an individual" (1983, p. 1366).

Major is defined as:

> "Serious or dangerous, requiring great attention or concern" (p. 787).

Both the autobiographical heuristic material and the informants' interviews made it perfectly clear that severe, profound trauma was a significant factor in precipitating one's arrival in the Underworld. It was also a consistent element of being present or remaining in the Underworld. Many participants experienced the same type of traumatic events in their lives, yet not all reacted the same way or at the same time. Some participants tolerated an accumulation of multiple stressors before they became overwhelmed and unable to cope. Others had intense responses to a defining event, although other traumatic sequelae were present in their lives. Close review of the interviews made it evident that the individuals' histories, psychological resiliency, and life experiences affected their perception of which negative event or events composed the major trauma that finally rendered them Emotionally Dead.

Susannah. For Susannah, the study's first participant, the road to the Underworld was a long time coming. She had lived a lifetime of mental illness, struggling with parents who did not understand and whose lack of support caused Susannah to feel negatively about herself. Multiple psychiatric hospitalizations, psychotropic prescriptions, and prolonged abuse of illicit street narcotics had taken their toll. Two crises which stood apart from a background already filled with despair were the death by suicide of her husband and being subjected to a brutal gang rape. In Susannah's own words, "No wonder I was dead. Would you like to feel this?" The human soul can encompass only so much suffering before it goes dead, numb, into shock, in order to allow the body to continue. For the soul to endure such pain would surely decrease the chances of keeping the body alive.

James. James noted the similar element of addiction in his past, his being alcoholism rather than polysubstance abuse. He also reported a less than satisfying marriage. Neither of these came forth as severe traumas for him. According to James, the single precipitating factor that sent him tumbling into the Underworld was the news of his wife leaving him and the accompanying grief over not having his son present with him on a permanent basis. This act was perceived by James as catastrophic, and caused him "the worst pain" he had ever felt in his life. His son was the focus of his world and for James, it brought up intense feelings of fear, abandonment, helplessness, and loneliness. In his own words, he "started thinking about drinking and knew . . . [he] was in trouble."

Frank. Frank also experienced one primary circumstance which sent him spiraling into the depths. The shock of being served with divorce papers by a process server he mistook for a client was astounding to Frank. He was completely unprepared for a trauma of such proportions, having already negotiated a drinking problem, a painfully estranged marriage, plummeting self-esteem, and a loss of Eros in his life. Being notified of the end of his world as he knew it was too much for Frank to contend with, and he went from "hysterical," to eventually "preparing . . . to die."

Mary. Mary related a history so riddled with trauma it was amazing she had not succumbed to the Underworld a very long time ago, and even more astonishing that she had been able to accomplish such a full and vital return to the Upperworld. Her trauma narrative included episodes of exclusion; parental alienation, rejection, and abandonment; the death of her father, whom she adored; being kicked out of her house as a minor and made to fend for herself; self-injurious behaviors of cutting, starving, and bulimia; poor treatment in a group home; homelessness; abusive relationships; rape; juvenile hall; and ultimately, the crowning blow, an unplanned pregnancy while still an adolescent living on the streets. As the self-doubt overtook her and her friends vanished, the Emotional Deadness took over. As Mary put it, "It was like I didn't exist."

Holly. Holly's interview also elicited a minefield of traumatic occurrences. It was nearly surreal hearing about the agonies the participants had lived through and how they somehow managed to "come to life again" after being crushed by the cruelties of the world. Holly's tragedies included being sick with chronic and potentially terminal illnesses, sitting with anticipatory grief while waiting for her best friend to die from a disease they shared, the unexpected death of her beloved brother, survivor guilt and bereavement grief after the passing of her loved ones, physical pain, and mourning the loss of what she had been able to do before she became ill. Although the death of her best friend Joe stood out as the main feature of her interview, it was very closely interwoven with the other incidents.

Summary. When considering *the lived experience of coming to life again after a period of emotional deadness*, one has to consider how it is that someone becomes Emotionally Dead to begin with. Traumatic events come in all shapes and sizes, in varying degrees of intensity and severity. All of the participants demonstrated the ability to withstand more than one injurious situation and hold their ground. For each interviewee, it took at least a foundation of some prior strain or stress to allow one massive event to cripple him or her, similar to an earthquake ripping open a crevasse along a fault line. This was the case for James and Frank, who could not metabolize the shock of their divorces; for Mary, who was stunned by an unplanned pregnancy; and for me, who was shocked by the overdose of my fiancé. For other participants, a combination of terrible events striking close together proved insurmountable. This occurred when Susannah's husband committed suicide, and she was gang raped within a very close period of time; and for Holly, who was struck with consecutive medical crises as well as consecutive deaths of significant others. The coping mechanisms are overwhelmed, and one slips down into the land of the Living Dead.

Alchemically, a major trauma would be a descent into the "blackness" (Jung, as cited in Kiehl, 2005, "Pathologizing Depression," para. 12), the world of the Shadow, where suffering is at home. Depression, Chaos, the Dragon, the Chthonic Spirit, the Devil, the Trickster, the Emotionally Dead: here is where they dwell. The alchemical cooking process occurs in stages which are circular in nature and may require many repetitions (Kiehl, 2005, "The Imaginal Realm of Depression," para. 12). This difficult and convoluted soul work would likely need a drop of "the living substance, blood, symbolized in the *rubedo*" (para. 13), to set its course in motion. A little bit of fire, a little bit of ash.

Great Pain

Great is defined by *The American Heritage Dictionary of the English Language* as:

> "a) Remarkable or outstanding in magnitude, degree, or extent; b) Significant, important, or meaningful; c) Powerful or influential" (1973, p. 576).

Pain is defined as:

> "a) An unpleasant sensation, occurring in varying degrees of severity as a consequence of injury, disease, or emotional disorder; b) Suffering or distress" (p. 942).

Experiencing unbearable pain on diverse levels was a key

Tales of Awakening

theme for each participant in *the lived experience of coming to life again after a period of emotional deadness.* The pain was described variously as *intense, intolerable,* and *unimaginable.* Participants experienced the pain as mental, emotional, spiritual, psychological, and physical. It was interesting that all the participants expressed feeling both Emotionally Dead and in insufferable pain. It is almost as if the only thing capable of penetrating the galactic numbness of the Emotionally Dead state is the bitter irony of Great Pain. This aspect of the experience presented itself somewhat differently for each participant.

Susannah. Susannah described the pain harrowingly as "pain so deep you want to take your own life." She speaks of a "complete emptiness, knowing only the feeling of sadness," which "becomes too much to bear." This mirrors the aforementioned state of deadness/numbness/emptiness other than a sense of pain/sadness/grief. Susannah alludes to the emotional torment thusly: "It would have been easier if they had just killed me."

James. James spoke of "the intense pain" of losing his child as being "the worst pain I ever felt in my life" and said he hoped "drinking would make the pain go away."

Frank. Frank described the rippling effect of the pain of betrayal, disappointment, confusion, shock, humiliation, and loss of his faith in God, and of lying awake at night contemplating his own suicide, eventually resorting to "whatever I could to numb the pain."

Mary. Mary divulged pain on all the dimensions noted previously, affectingly referring to her maltreated adolescent self in sad, pejorative terms: "I was an idiot, a loser, dumb, vulnerable, stupid. . . " She remembers times of terror, and of feeling completely alone. Speaking of her father's death, she said, "The pain ate at me."

Holly. Holly also endured Great Pain on various levels, with considerable amounts being physical and a great deal of her emotional pain experienced corporeally as well. Holly lived with the chronic, daily distress of an auto-immune disease, the postoperative discomfort of an organ transplant, the psychological pain of depression, and tremendous psychic and embodied pain surrounding grief and bereavement matters. For Holly, quite simply, "Pain is hell."

Summary. As the participants share their experiences, we see that pain can be viewed from many different angles: the literal physical pain of illness or injury, the psychic pain of depression, the emotional pain of rejection or abandonment, the spiritual pain of betrayal or lost faith, and the numb pain of emptiness. It is the grim paradox of Emotional Deadness that one can somehow feel dead and yet be in pain at the same time. Pain can be seen as part of both the alchemical blackening and reddening stages, burning and searing its way through the deadness, branding the soul with evidence of the trip to the dark abyss.

Tales of Awakening

Loss or Separation

The American Heritage Dictionary of the English Language (1973) defines loss:

> a) The harm or suffering caused by losing or by being lost, b) Casualties"; coming from *lost*, meaning "a) Strayed or missing; b) Gone in time, passed away; c) Gone morally astray, fallen [here is evidence of the stigma regarding the Underworld]; d) Bewildered; e) Unable to function, act, or make progress; helpless. (p. 771)

Separation is defined as:

> "a) The place where a division or parting occurs; b) An interval or space that separates; a gap" (p. 1181).

To separate is defined as:

> a) To set or keep apart; divide; disunite. b) To space apart. c) To differentiate or discriminate between. d) To remove, isolate. e) To part. f) To become disconnected or severed; come apart; part. g) To withdraw. h) To part company. i) To become divided. j) Set apart from the rest; not connected; disjointed; detached. k) Withdrawn from others; solitary; isolated. l) Dissimilar; distinct. m) Not shared; individual. (p. 1181)

All of the participants experienced some form of separation, estrangement, or loss. The situations were as varied as a loss of one's former abilities, a loss of health, and the death of a partner. Just like Inanna, who lost all her worldly belongings piece by piece and entered the Underworld naked and helpless, the participants in this study lost things of vital importance until they felt completely bereft.

Susannah. Susannah's losses, like so many others, came in multiples: a loss of self-worth and self-esteem from her mental illness and the way her parents dealt with it, a loss of positive self-regard from her chemical dependency, a loss of the will to live stemming from her brutal rape, and the loss of her husband to suicide. She said, "The hardest thing is coming to terms with someone you love taking their own life. That isn't supposed to happen."

James. While undergoing a marital separation, James was undone not by the loss of his marriage or his wife, but by the awareness that he would be separated from his son. He was in profound pain over the thought of the potential split to the point where it was all he could think about: "I was losing my baby . . . losing my child."

Frank. Frank felt the loss of Eros in his marriage when he and his wife became more like "business partners." Next went his loss of self-worth when he felt "belittled" in comparison to his wife's new friends. Ultimately, he lost his actual wife and son: "I missed her dearly and missed my son beyond comprehension."

Mary. Mary's interview exemplifies layer upon layer of loss: loss of her childhood and adolescence, her home, her parents, her sense of safety and belonging in the world, and finally, control over her own body when she discovered she was a child who was going to have a child. She lost friends literally and figuratively. Once-in-a-lifetime opportunities were gone. "I had lost out on so much in life. I fucked up...again."

Holly. Loss was a major focal point for Holly. She lost her health and, with it, her faith that she could rely on her own body to do what it was supposed to do, what it had done previously. She lost her best friend and her brother, both integral components of her support system. Her health issues and her best friend's death prompted a loss of trust in the medical community and in God, who were seen as either fallible or vengeful. The extremity of loss was summarized by Holly: "I made a game out of measuring my losses against their victories."

Summary. As evidenced in the review of myths and fairy tales, the journey to the Underworld is precipitated or accompanied by some form of loss or estrangement. *Snow White* (Seifert, 1986) nearly loses her life to the evil Queen before she falls into her deep stupor, not quite dead but far from alive. She loses her freedom of movement and experiencing, while she is suspended in the netherworld of the Glass Coffin.

Inanna (Henderson & Oakes, 1963) loses her 14 powers one by one. She enters the Underworld naked and defenseless. She is judged, condemned, abused, and hung on a hook like a cadaver. No one is there to help her; she is alone. Likewise, the participants in this study were summarily stripped of their defenses and their precious attachments, be they people, health, homes, sanity, love, or faith. They were reduced to mere shadows of their former selves, walking the streets nameless and faceless, like Mary and her infant; driving blindly through a watershed of tears, like James; or dissolving into a drunken pile in a bar, like Frank. The losses were so powerful they took away not only the will to live but the sense of actually *being alive.* From an alchemical viewpoint, loss and estrangement also produce a potent pang of redness when the wound is fresh, scabbing over into blackness to seal the hole.

Isolation or Exclusion

A sense of isolation or exclusion was common to all the participants. *The American Heritage Dictionary of the English Language* (1973) defines *isolate* as:

> "a) To separate from a group or whole and set apart. b) To place in quarantine. c) To obtain a substance in an uncombined form" (p. 694).

Here is seen the alchemical possibility of an individual being removed from the world of the living in order to become *prima materia.* From this basest of places begins the work of the *coniunctio* in order to emerge eventually as *The Philosopher's Stone. Exclude* is defined as:

> "a) To prevent or keep from entering a place, group, or the like; to bar; reject. b) To omit noticing or considering; leave out; disregard. c) To put out (someone or something); expel" (p. 458).

The participants in this study all made reference to feeling isolated or excluded from the rest of the world, which sometimes prefaced their time in the Underworld or was experienced during their time in it. For some, the feeling remained even after their return, in a somewhat altered fashion. They were part of the Upperworld again, but not quite the same as everyone else. Their experience of *coming to life again after a period of Emotional Deadness* forever changed them. How this element affected each participant is explored further.

Susannah. "My family is always comparing me to someone who functions better than me...No one truly understands my troubles but me." Susannah's sense of being judged by others and found to be "less than" or "damaged goods" haunted her during her darkest days. So much of what she identified as "her" made her feel different, such as having a mental illness and having been raped. This was compounded by other people's reactions to her (doctors, parents), which reinforced her perception of being alone in her journey. The loss of her spouse was a major factor in Susannah feeling isolated, because she felt it was a pain few could understand and "it's not supposed to happen."

James. After James became separated from his wife and child, he went through a period of total withdrawal. He went to work and back, his head filled only with thoughts of losing his son and whether drinking could kill the pain. He had no connection to the outside world on an emotional level. At first, James tried to contend with his experience alone, feeling adrift and inconsolable. He blocked out the external world as much as possible. He said,

"I drove through Hidden Valley with tears squirting out of my eyes, just like in the cartoons."

James knew about the dangers of isolating from his experience as a recovering alcoholic: "I knew I was in trouble. . . . I knew I had to take action soon so I found out what time my old favorite meetings were taking place and where." James was fortunate in that his period of isolation lasted only a month. He did not perceive himself as excluded prior to the separation or after he sought help. This may be due to James's personality type being less depth- and insight-oriented or to the comfort and support he received in his AA meetings.

Frank. For Frank, isolation and exclusion were bitter realities that seemed to spiral out of control. His shock, despair, humiliation, and inability to cope with the unforeseen departure of his wife and son left him fragmented. He no longer could relate to the friends he had had during his marriage. Except for brief visits with his child, Frank was a solo act: "I withdrew from my friends, my family, and life. I just didn't care about life anymore."

Mary. Coming from a marginalized multicultural ethnic and religious background led to Mary feeling isolated and excluded from an early age. She was made to feel "not the norm" by others who were intolerant of diversity or at best uncouth about their lack of familiarity with her family's ancestry and traditions. She was rejected by her mother after her father passed away, which affected their relationship and her personality development.

Mary believed she was shunned by society, based on a lack of belief in her own right to belong instilled by her mother's view of her as "an abomination."

Holly. Holly felt isolated and excluded from her own body and from a world outside of the hospital. Regarding her experiences of anticipatory grief, death, dying, and bereavement, she described the feeling of being trapped in the Underworld in explicit terms, lending it a kinesthetic portraiture. "It was difficult to see the sunshine from the bottom of that well because it was a dark, demoralizing, and heavy place. . . . For me, the well was dry...I believe I was at the bottom, both emotionally, and physically." It is hard to imagine *not* having a sentiment of isolation and exclusion existing in such a desolate space.

Summary. Linking back to the presence of isolation and exclusion as an element in myth and fairy tale, Snow White is found sequestered from the world in the coffin the dwarves have prepared for her (Seifert, 1986). She is in suspension, neither alive nor dead, but not a part of the world around her. Persephone very dramatically becomes segregated from her mother Demeter and all who dwell above ground when Hades kidnaps her and holds her captive in the Underworld (Strong, 2000). Inanna, Queen of Heaven and Earth, is trapped in the lair of her dangerous sister Ereshkigal, Queen of the Underworld, and is turned into a rotting corpse (Elder, 2001).

Although these are all frightening and desolate times for

these archetypal figures as well as the study participants, alchemically, the period of isolation and seclusion, the pain of the *rubedo*, and the deadness of the *nigredo* are necessary to moving on. So it is in Jungian or depth psychology: one must go down into the unconscious and the Shadow in order to individuate and later *mine the gold in the shadow* (Sharp, 1991).

Betrayal

Betrayal was a theme common to all the interviewees in this study. Like the other themes that have been examined, betrayal occurred on disparate levels and in sometimes unordinary ways. Betrayal ranged from romantic treachery to parental unfaithfulness, to spiritual let-down, and to the disloyalty of one's own body.

The American Heritage Dictionary of the English Language (1973) defines *betray* as:

> "a) to be disloyal or faithless to; b) to deceive" (p. 128).

Betrayal plays an integral role in the Underworld leitmotifs already analyzed. It was often the major trauma, it always caused great pain, it was certainly experienced as a loss or estrangement, and it led to feelings of isolation or exclusion. Among the participants, the array of bio-psycho-socio-emotional injuries left in the wake of betrayal was multifaceted.

Tales of Awakening

Susannah. Susannah's interview contained no end of betrayals, some more damaging than others. She felt betrayed by her own mind when her Bi-polar Disorder took over, by the medical community when she was hospitalized involuntarily, by her parents when they made comparisons and found her lacking compared to others, by her husband when he took his own life, and by the universe as a whole when she was gang raped. Her lack of safety or trust after being so deceived by the external world was made clear by her statement, "This is when I should learn to become my own best friend." She had to learn how to trust and rely on herself first and then practice it. She also had to become aware of how others preyed on her for being so trusting: "I do have a tendency to trust people too easily, then somehow they hurt me."

James. James's Underworld pilgrimage was initiated when his wife stated that she was leaving him, had met someone else, and was not coming back. James explained:

> The day she told me she wanted a separation, the worst day of my life. . . . I had hoped the whole time that we would get back together so I could be with my son all the time again, then she informed me that she had found someone else and I realized that my son wouldn't be coming back—I drove through Hidden Valley that day crying so hard that tears were squirting out of my eyes (just like in the cartoons).

The sense of dashed hopes, wishes and dreams unfulfilled, plotting behind his back, and being caught off guard spelled out betrayal for James.

Frank. Interpersonal and spiritual betrayals were central factors in Frank's dark depression. Being double-crossed by someone he trusted led to Frank feeling betrayed by God as well as his wife. He knew his marriage was less than perfect, but he never imagined it was unhappy enough for his spouse to leave him suddenly, without warning, and take his child. The sense of being taken by surprise by another's duplicity is evident in Frank's interview:

> The process server pulled divorce papers out of his briefcase and told me Katie had filed for divorce. I was shocked. . . . I was stunned. I then knew something was horribly wrong. How could someone who said they loved me and vowed to spend the rest of their life with me do this to me? I was hoping this whole nightmare would come to an end. How could God do this to me? How could my wife do this to me?

Mary. Relationship betrayal was familiar ground for Mary from childhood on. She was betrayed inadvertently by her father when he passed away, which was compounded by her mother's intentional betrayal of refusing to nurture, support, and protect her minor child. She was betrayed by many of the people and places that should have safeguarded her, such as the juvenile hall and the Christian group home where she was sent. Her years on the streets were filled with betrayal, from her closest partner to strangers. Her boyfriend betrayed her by stealing from her and by not being true to his word. Her trust was violated by being mugged, abandoned by friends, and being left to fend for herself. Her desperation and history made her vulnerable to being betrayed by some figures (her mother, her boyfriend) repeatedly. Her world was so harsh that revictimization was her norm, not an anomaly. Mary stated:

> Father . . . died a very unexpected death . . . my mother did not like me . . . getting kicked out of home . . . all of the people who said they were my friends no longer cared. . . . I was terrified to ask anyone for help and those I did ask turned a blind eye to my existence. . . . I was abused by my baby's father. It started when I was pregnant. He dragged me by the hair once when I went following him to the corner where he bought his crack. The crack dealer just stood there laughing and howling at me while the boy kicked me and punched me. I was always getting into trouble looking for that boy. Once I had to leave my baby with strangers, punk rock kids I had just met, so I could find that boy. He left with my last five dollars to buy formula—I had to stop nursing 'cause I was sick—and didn't come back. I waited almost 2 days. ... While wandering around L.A. looking for him, I came across some guys with masks . . . it was Halloween . . . who acted like they knew me . . . said my guy was coming right back. . . . What a fool I was . . . I didn't listen to my intuition . . . I got mugged. . . What a dummy. I digress.   Finally he left for good. He went on a binge and took all my savings. The entire lot of it, $300. That was it, all I had. Once again, I was screwed.

Holly. The theme of betrayal was prominent in Holly's interview. She described incidents of being victimized in many aspects of her life. These various blows caused her to struggle with skepticism and uncertainty about the world around her. Holly felt emotionally hijacked by these ordeals and reacted with anger, anxiety, despair, confusion, frustration, and fear, depending on the circumstances. For Holly, betrayal could range from her own body not functioning properly to someone else receiving inadequate medical care, an indirect act that caused a direct reaction and response, for it meant the loss of a dear friend to a painful death. At times, Holly even felt betrayed by God, which is not unusual and has appeared in other participants' interviews and autobiographical material (e.g., Frank asking "How could God do this to me?"). Holly recalled,

> It seemed to me as if everything in my life was being destroyed. The early start of summer, in 2004, I started having symptoms. 2003 was the darkest I'd ever faced, my brother died and my health tumbled. I was certain someone up there hated me. At the same time I expressed my hatred for Joe's primary care physician. It was then that I realized I might have to make a decision. Do I continue to loathe and condemn him for not finding the cancer sooner? The signs were definitely there and he neglected to act upon his findings. I was so infuriated. He could have started chemo and radiation, then there were discussions back in October about a liver transplant, which never transpired 'cause Joe's PCP [primary care physician] waited too long to refer him to a specialist. On the other hand, it would have been more time he spent sick and scared. Or, do I thank God, who I've hated for so many months, that the people who love Joe had to watch cancer ravage him? Pain is hell . . . most of the day what I felt was a physical pain. The best I can describe it is to liken it to when your foot falls asleep. Imagine that feeling in your chest. Then when you move your foot to wake it up—the shooting pain you feel. Imagine that feeling in your chest all day long. That's what it felt like.

Summary. In the alchemical framework, betrayal again appears to belong to the *rubedo/nigredo* stage of the process for the participants as well as archetypally. When one first learns of being betrayed by a trusted other, there is normally a flash of hot emotion: fury, despair, rage, tears, and so forth. The mood can also be cold: disgust, desire for revenge, and hatred. One may shift from the reddening into the blackness of the scarred, old wound or the blackness may become heated when confronted by an object which reignites the feelings surrounding the discovery of the betrayal.

Emotional Deadness

The American Heritage Dictionary of the English Language (1973) defines *emotion* as:

> "a) Agitation of the passions or sensibilities often involving physiological changes. b) Any strong feeling, as of joy, sorrow, reverence, hate, or love, arising subjectively rather than through conscious mental effort" (p. 428).

Dead is defined as:

> a) No longer alive; lifeless. b) Not having the capacity to live; inanimate. c) Lacking feeling or sensitivity; unresponsive. d) No longer in existence, force, use, or operation. e) Devoid of animation, interest, or excitement. f) Not productive, idle. g) Weary and worn-out; exhausted. h) Without brightness or luster. i) Without resonance. j) Extinguished. k) Lacking elasticity or resilience. l) Out of play. m) Lacking connection to a source of electric current; drained of electric charge; discharged. n) No longer needed for use. o) The period of greatest intensity. (p. 338)

Descriptions and examples of emotional deadness from the participants' interviews, mythology, and fairy tales have been included in the preceding subthemes of the Underworld. My own autobiographical heuristic experience presented in Chapter 3 touches upon the definition noted above. It was a time of the peculiar oxymoron of *intense nothingness*. The world was hollow; I was brittle and friable. I operated in the world like a moving Snow White in her glass coffin (Seifert, 1986); everything was just out of reach, and nothing could reach me because of the invisible wall. Like living underwater and forgetting to come back up for air, something failed to spark, but I was already too oxygen-deficient to understand what was happening, much less fix it.

Alchemically, the *rubedo* present in the Underworld may even be viewed symbolically in the blood red fruit of the Pomegranate which ensures Persephone's captivity with Hades (Strong, 2000) in the achromatic *nigredo*. It appears again in Snow White's drops of blood on the snow, the poisoned red apple, and her bright red lips (Seifert, 1986). Christ bleeds red on his cross of darkness. The Phoenix rises brightly from the grayness of the ashes. The *nigredo* of the Underworld presents in the darkness of Kore's descent into the world of the dead (Orbis, 2007), Demeter's barren Upperworld (Strong, 2000), Inanna's transformation into a corpse (Elder, 2001), Christ's wounds scabbing, Christ dying, the Phoenix dying, and the many shades of black in Snow White (Seifert, 1986): the death of the Queen, the ebony windows, Snow White's ebony hair, the dark ground in which the dwarves refuse to bury her, and her period of lifeless suspension.

The Turning Point: Crisis/Intervention

The American Heritage Dictionary of the English Language (1973) defines *crisis* as:

> a) A crucial point or situation in the course of anything; turning point; b) An unstable condition . . . in which an abrupt or decisive change is impending; c) A sudden change in the course of an acute disease, either toward improvement or deterioration; d) The point in a story or drama at which hostile forces are in the most tense state of opposition. (p. 314)

Intervene is defined as:

> "a) To enter or occur extraneously; b) To come, appear, or lie between two things; c) To occur or come between two periods or points of time; d) To come in between so as to hinder or modify" (p. 686).

The interjection or appearance of an intervention allows the crisis to set the stage for transformation. The appropriate intermediation at the proper time results in the transfiguration back toward life. It is at this juncture that the impetus for change and growth is possible. This is the "do or die" stage where something reaches a boiling point, the status quo is shaken up by an unexpected intervention, or the system remains a closed loop without the opportunity for transformation and renewed progression. In the interviews and personal accounts contained herein, significant events resulted in new courses of action for participants, specifically, the drive toward survival and return to living.

Susannah. Susannah's insight came in the form of a class on Posttraumatic Stress Disorder which provided her with several important factors: an understanding of what had happened to her, why it had affected her as it did, and what she could do to cope with the lasting effects of her assault; the sense of validation that she was normal; and the comfort that she was not alone. Here, she became conscious enough to make the decision to hurt herself or help herself, and bravely, she chose to help herself.

James. James awoke to his crisis point when he realized he was thinking about drinking "to make the pain go away." He had become conscious enough to realize that he was on treacherous ground for a recovering alcoholic and that he needed to make a choice to get help or slip back into his old disease. James was sufficiently unsettled by his thinking to reach out for assistance and begin to climb back toward the Upperworld with newfound support and encouragement.

Frank. The crisis point came to a head when Frank passed out in a bar, a drunken shadow of his former self. The once proud and happy family man had reached his all-time low and was obliterated by alcohol. His intervention came in the form of a significant other —two in fact—watching out for him. The local bartender took pity on him and called a friend of his rather than the police, and the friend ran to Frank's rescue, his "knight in shining armor" figure. This gesture enabled Frank to recognize how unmanageable his situation had become, but also gave him hope to try to get well because he saw that people still cared about him even when he had lost the ability to care about himself.

Mary. Life hit a pinnacle crisis point for Mary when living on the streets once again had her at rock bottom. Out of money, energy, friends, and hope, she was ready to break. Fate intervened through the good fortune of her normally rejecting mother finally offering her some support and shelter again. Mary was ready and willing to grasp the chance to get her life together, even if it meant living with the parent who ostracized her then and now. She was able to allow gratitude toward her mother and concern for her infant to outweigh the shame of being treated like a social pariah. Although she admits she felt like a "loser" collecting welfare, she now was "humbled" by motherhood's new responsibilities and found herself on an upward path.

Holly. Holly's crisis was very spiritual and internal in nature. She suddenly had a moment where the Serenity Prayer made deep sense to her and gave her something to hold on to. It was a life jacket that kept her afloat when she was drowning, metaphorically speaking. It made sense to her in a practical, applicable way that she could use to contend with life's hardships and disappointments. Her perception of the prayer and how to interpret and apply it changed over time as she became stronger. At first, it gave her the peace to accept the tragedies she had no ability to control; later it gave her the courage to start making changes where she could be effective. This prayer was a small version of the grieving manual she had been missing during her time in the Underworld.

The formerly silent, black-and-white world Holly had perceived began to appear in sound and color. She noticed the blooming of flowers, the melting of snow, and the sounds of the world alive and in bloom around her. These things were there all along, but while she was in the Underworld, they were as if nonexistent. The awakening began subtly, but built momentum as the small gains brought increasing relief and joy. After becoming aware of the natural world, Holly's attention broadened to encompass her son and her hobbies as other sources of vitality and liveliness. The more she was able to take in, the greater became her openness to positive, healing emotions of gratitude, forgiveness, wisdom, and appreciation. She stated, "I realized I had all the things my brother wanted . . . and I woke up each morning in the presence of someone who loved me."

Summary

The Turning Point marks the first positioning away from

the Underworld and out of the state of Emotional Deadness. It is here that the participants and I experienced the phenomenological aspect of the initial sparks of *coming to life again*. Whether by some internal shift affording clarity and vision, an external opportunity to regroup, a savior figure lifting one up from the depths, hitting "rock bottom" and desiring a different way of life, or finding oneself in a class that provides insight and removes stigma, participants shared the common experience of a sense of awakening. This awakening was felt as purpose, direction, movement, and a new paradigm or view of the world and one's experiences in it.

From an alchemical perspective, this can be seen as movement out of the *rubedo* and *nigredo* of the Underworld and into the *albedo* of the "in between" portion of the journey. The crisis moments would likely still be "red" and "black," so to speak: moments of rude awakenings, shocking realizations, tough choices, hard decisions, and fortitude which are not for the faint of heart. The intervention element clearly is inseparable from the crisis; however, it offers the first glimpses of hope, possibility, renewed faith, and aspirations for a better outcome, hence the appearance of the *albedo* or whitening of consciousness.

The Transformation: Painful Awakening/Taking Action

The American Heritage Dictionary of the English

Language (1973) defines *transform* as:

> "a) To change markedly the form or appearance of;
> b) To change the nature, function, or condition of; to
> convert; c) To undergo a transformation" (p. 1363).

The key components or themes of the Transformation Stage for the participants were Awakening and Action. These processes sometimes occurred concurrently and, at other times, consecutively. For some participants, Awakening enabled Action to occur; for others taking Action led to an Awakening.

Awakening is defined as:

> a) Waking up; b) Rousing; c) Exciting; d) The act of
> waking; an emergence from sleep; e) A stirring up; a
> rousing of attention or interest" (p. 92). Action is defined as
> "a) The state or process of acting or doing; condition of
> being active; b) An act or deed; c) A movement or series of
> movements; d) Activity, energy; e) Behavior or conduct; f)
> The transmission of energy, force, or influence; g) Any
> change that occurs in the body or in a bodily organ as a
> result of its functioning; h) The series of events and episodes
> that form the plot of a story or play; i) *the appearance of
> animation of a figure in painting or sculpture* [italics added;
> reminiscent of an inanimate object becoming animate, i.e.,
> a dead object coming to life]. (p. 13)

Susannah. Susannah described her awakening as terribly painful yet ultimately opening her up to a greater level of acceptance, increased spirituality, and a miraculous new life. The appearance of her deceased husband in the form of a blue jay was the key to Susannah's awakening. This moment renewed and strengthened her spirituality and helped her to heal. Her increased spiritual faith gave her the courage and strength to begin addressing and combating many of the other long-standing difficulties in her life, such as her abuse and addiction. Interestingly, Susannah uses action words to describe her way from the Underworld to the Upperworld: "coming through to the other side," "the end of the road," and "allow[ing] flow . . . to lead you on your journey." Again, sometimes one actually takes a specific action or actions, other times the phenomenon is experienced as having a quality of movement on a gestalt level.

James. James's Underworld and Turning Point stages were nearly unbearable for him. His Transformation stage was an intricate mix of Awakening and Action intertwined, making it an interactive process where each breakthrough fostered an advance in the next area. James had a spiritual awakening and a deeply powerful moment of healing when he received the loving support he had hoped for from the other men at the AA meeting, yet it had taken some action to get him there, which in turn had come from his awakening to the fact that he was in trouble because he was thinking about drinking to kill his pain. In many of the interviews, this interweaving of Action/Awakening/Action/Awakening can be seen quite clearly or teased out with closer examination.

James took many practical actions in addition to attending meetings: he called other men from the program and kept in touch with them, he began reading spiritual literature daily, he practiced thought-stopping when a negative thought crossed his mind, he began listening to music at work to distract himself from upsetting thoughts, and he started to exercise on a regular basis. As he described it, the more awake he became, the more actions he felt capable of taking; the more actions he felt compelled to take, the more awake he became. This productive cycle propels movement toward the Upperworld.

Frank. Frank's primary awakening during his trans-formation stage was the realization that his depression was triggered by his divorce and in turn fueled by his alcoholism. He took the immediate action of becoming sober and followed it with many other actions as his newfound clarity of thinking allowed him more profound insights, which in turn propelled Frank toward more useful courses of action. He pursued legal and physical custody of his son, he went to church due to his renewed faith and spirituality, and he joined a faith-based group for single parents. Here, he had another huge awakening, realizing that he was not alone in his dilemma and that he had undergone a universal experience, which actually made him feel closer to God and other people instead of isolated and estranged. He felt more forgiving, healed, and whole once he had this insight, which came as a result of his having taken an action. He also realized his health was in jeopardy, and he began to exercise and eat well, which also improved his mood, thinking, decision-making, and future action-taking.

Mary. Mary's transformational stage was again a richly interwoven texture of cause and effect. She took the action of moving out of her mother's house to a new city and joining a band. This action led to her awakening to the fact that she was gifted with the ability to entertain others as a musician and performer, a gift and talent she had long forgotten she possessed. A plethora of awakenings and realizations stemmed from this rediscovery of her identity as a gifted, talented person. Mary gained deeper and more profound awakenings. She realized that she still had a tremendous amount of work ahead of her and that much knowledge was still to be gained and much to be learned; yet every awakening and action made her feel like she had already put the worst of it behind her and would be able to face with courage and fortitude what life put in her path from then on.

Holly. Holly's transformation phase was very full. First, she took the action of reaching out to a co-worker for some words of support and advice. This co-worker served as a transformational figure, being the proverbial right person with the right words at the right place and time. He encouraged her to go explore and play, which opened up a new world for Holly besides one filled with grief, pain, loss, and suffering. She found herself newly opening to healing inspiration, gaining insight, facing fear, and navigating the unknown. Holly's spiritual faith became much like my own, which is basically the belief that everything happens for a reason, and there is a reason for everything that happens, even if it is beyond our ability to comprehend at the time we experience it. This spiritual foundation gave her a remarkable amount of courage literally to explore the world, even though she was ill and alone. She took hikes, rode her motorcycle on long trips, drove her sports car on unplanned outings, and became quite fearless in the world.

Summary

The Transformational phase as experienced by the participants illustrates quite poignantly the intertwining of the Jungian individuation process and the alchemical progression away from the *nigredo* and *rubedo* into the *albedo* and towards the *Sol*. The alchemical symbolism of transforming the lead of Saturn into the golden *Sol* of new consciousness is well on its way in the Transformation phase. The process occurs in stages, many times repetitious, often circular in nature, and ultimately endless. As Jung states, the work of individuation is difficult, dangerous, and strewn with obstacles, and so it is with the alchemical opus, which includes struggle, mystery, suffering, disappearance, the synthesis of opposites, the assimilation of shadow, and the integration of evil. The soul, however, struggles to express itself through the whitening of conscious recognition of the lived experience. As the Transformation stage leads back to life and the

Upperworld, one can already see and feel the slivers of golden *Sol* shining through the opus and lighting the path for the survivors.

The Upperworld:

Telling the Story and Sharing the Trauma, New Life and New

Identity

The American Heritage Dictionary of the English Language (1973) defines the word *tell* as follows:

> a) To give a detailed account of; narrate; recount; b) To communicate by speech or writing; express with words; c) To make known to; notify, inform; d) To make known; reveal; disclose; e) To give an account, enumeration, or description; f) To give evidence or indication; g) To have an effect or impact. (p. 1324)

Share is defined as:

> "a) To participate in, use, or experience in common; b) To have or take a part, participate; join" (p. 1191).

Story is defined as:

> a) The narrating or relating of an event or series of events, either true or fictitious; b) A prose or verse narrative, usually fictional, intended to interest or amuse the hearer or reader; a tale; c) A report, statement, or allegation of the facts; d) An anecdote; e) Romantic legend or tradition. (p. 1271)

New is defined as:

> a) Of recent origin; having existed only a short time; lately made produced, or grown; b) Not yet old, fresh; recent; c) Used for the first time, not secondhand; d)

Recognized or experienced lately for the first time, although existing before, recently become known; e) Freshly introduced, unfamiliar, unaccustomed; f) Begun afresh; g) Newly entered into a state, position, or experience; h) Changed for the better; refreshed, rejuvenated; h) Different and distinct from what was before; i) In the most recent form, period, or development of something. (p. 884)

Life is defined as:

a) The property or quality manifested in functions such as metabolism [integration and assimilation of opposites], growth [individuation], response to stimulation [disintegration or transformation] and reproduction, by which *living organisms are distinguished from dead organisms or from inanimate matter* [italics added]; b) The characteristic state or condition of a living organism; c) A living being, especially a person, contrasted with one no longer alive; d) The interval between the birth or inception of an organism and its death; e) The interval or amount of time during which anything exists or functions; f) A spiritual state regarded as a transcending of death. g) An account of a person's life; a biography; h) Human activities, relationships, and interests collectively; i) A manner of activity or a characteristic of existence; j) An animating force; a source of vitality; k) animation, spirit, or liveliness; l) Strength or freshness of flavor; m) Actual environment or reality; nature; n) To cause to regain consciousness; o) To put spirit into; to animate; p) To make lifelike; q) To regain consciousness; r) To become animated; grow lively; s) desperately or urgently; t) So as to save one's life. (p. 754)

Finally, *identity* is defined as:

a) The collective aspect of the set of characteristics by which a thing is definitively recognizable or known; b) The set of behavioral or personal characteristics by which an individual is recognizable as a member of a group; d) The quality or condition of being or remaining the same; e) the personality of an individual regarded as a persisting entity. (p. 654)

For Susannah, the final stage of her alchemical opus was filled with the realization that "life is what you make of it," that she "really was a survivor," that she felt empowered by telling her story to others, and that she had a strong sense of having become a "living legacy," a person who now represented and advocated for her deceased husband who was no longer here to represent himself. Susannah expressed that these were not just perceived as new layers or additions to her sense of self but were actually experienced as a new identity or personhood, leaving her with different life concepts, viewpoints, and vocational endeavors than had existed previously.

James. For James, the Upperworld was experienced in slowly coming out of his intense pain and regaining a sense of life and, in coming to life again, a feeling of gratitude for being alive when he might otherwise have literally been dead. Again, the parallel to not only an awakening but a new life, identity, and perspective of gratitude are key factors in James's return to the world of those who have found the Philosopher's Stone.

Frank. Frank's Upperworld rebirth consisted of drastic changes in his self-care routine due to his profoundly altered outlook on life.

Other changes were his newfound awareness of supportive family and friends, his intensely deep investment in being a parent and watching his son mature, and his sudden ability to look forward to his future rather than dreading it and hoping it would never come. His perception of his growth, hopefulness, and gratitude were both qualitatively and quantitatively different after his coming to life again from a period of emotional deadness. He felt like a new person, a different man. The *coniunctio* had taken place.

Mary. Mary described her return to the Upperworld as "A New Life." She suddenly found herself in many roles she had never experienced before in the Underworld. Mary spoke of being a teacher, a successful parent, a popular entertainer with a thriving career, and finally having a good relationship and stable housing for the first time in her life. Internally, she felt filled with wisdom, gratitude, forgiveness, hope, and wholeness. She felt blessed, healed, empowered, and that her experiences had been destined as a journey of self-discovery. Mary had come full circle, from the frightened, sheltered, timid child she once was, into a woman fully in control of her own power. The alchemical vessel had completed its work.

Holly. Holly's new life and new identity were described fully. She said that in hindsight, the wait was easy to talk about but excruciatingly difficult actually to linger through. She had come to realize that life had its challenges, but it also had its gifts. Her ability to survive had resulted in an increase in her confidence level. She developed a new sense of connection by forming friendships with others in similar situations. Her "un-normality" became normalized by seeking out others with afflictions and struggles so that she no longer felt isolated and alone. Holly transformed her painful and depressing experiences into something positive by using them to help others who were suffering; she became a "wounded healer" who could be of service and "pay it forward."

Additionally, Holly had newfound patience and discovered tools which helped her cope with the challenges she had to face. She incorporated these into her new life in the Upperworld and felt they maintained her ability to stay there and not sink below again. These tools included activity and involvement in her community; practicing good personal hygiene, self-education and awareness, and exercise; avoiding self-pity; monitoring her body language; distracting herself from upsetting thoughts; making time to play; getting help when she knew she needed it; and telling her story, a key component to wellness. All of these things helped her to live in the *Sol*, the new consciousness.

Structural Description of Coming to Life Again After a Period of Emotional Deadness

The experience of coming to life again after a period of emotional deadness, though somewhat variable for each individual who makes such a difficult journey, involves certain key themes or components which remain stable from participant to participant. The journey begins in by entering the Underworld due to some form of great pain, loss, separation, betrayal, isolation, or exclusion. After suffering this type of major trauma, those who do make their way back develop or discover temporary coping mechanisms such as self-medicating or self-deprecation. Next, they encounter a turning point in the form of a crisis and an intervention, often in the form of another person entering the scene. This leads to a personal transformation of an awakening, frequently spiritual in nature, a sense of healing, and the taking of some kind of action. Finally, in the Upperworld, these individuals experience a sense of a new life and a new identity, often propelled by the act of sharing their traumas or telling their stories to others.

Poststructural Discussion

The process of coming alive again after a period of emotional deadness is not experienced by the participants as a linear process. The various aspects of the experience work in conjunction with each other, interacting, supporting, and reinforcing the stages of individuation and alchemical processing. The phenomenological experience cannot be laid out upon a grid in neat, clean, concise steps. A tremendous amount of overlap and blurred boundaries exists between some of the stages of progression; certain themes such as self-medicating appeared in more than one subcategory of the metaphorical journey. For some participants, self-medicating was present in the underworld as part of their demise; for others, it was the crux of their turning point, when they finally realized they had a problem; and for some, it lingered into the transformation stage, when they were attempting to try new roles and ways of being in the world while needing somehow to take the edge off their newly awakened pain.

The phenomenological experience of coming to life again after a period of emotional deadness, as a human act, is tightly intertwined with the field of depth and archetypal psychology, the history of alchemy, and the realm of mythology, literature, and fairy tale. Without human saga, there can be no stories, and without stories to tell from generation to generation, there is not much to pass along in human culture. All the suffering and the struggles must have some meaning, or the random cruelty would be too much to bear. Have the myths, legends, and fairy tales helped us to give meaning to our pain, or has our struggle to give meaning to our pain resulted in the collective body of myths, legends, and fairy tales?

Differing Approaches to Myth and Its Service

Why . . .

have a yearning for destiny?. . .

because being here amounts to so much, because all this Here and Now, so fleeting, seems to require us and strangely concerns us. Us the most fleeting of all. . . .

Having been once on earth—can it ever be cancelled?

Heidi Elowitch (Taylor)

—Rainer Maria Rilke, "The Ninth Duino Elegy"

(as cited in Hollis, 1995, p. 7)

Just as religious faith obliges one to wait with trust in the mystery, so the evolution of the personality the individuation urge toward wholeness, obliges one to wait upon, and trust the guidance of, the soul's energies. The enemy of such trust is the anxiety caused by ambiguity. As one matures, a greater tolerance of ambiguity is essential both for growth and as a measure of respect for the autonomy of the mystery. *Myth is the dramatization of conscious or unconscious values of a group or an individual.* A relationship to the past (time as *chronos)* enables one to participate also in the eternal (time as *Kairos)*. Reading myth, then, is a form of personal and cultural psychotherapy (Greek *psyche,* soul, and *therapeuein,* to listen or attend to). Thus psychotherapy, whether it takes place in an analyst's office or in the mindful attention to one's inner life, is "listening to the soul." The recurrent motifs of myth constitute the movement of soul through the ages and through the life of the individual. (Hollis, 1995, pp. 11-23)

For the participants in this study, it was both typical as well as helpful for them to find some type of meaning in their journey and to be able to identify positive gifts that they had been granted out of their trials. As William Blake stated, "we must more consciously create our own myth or be enslaved to the myth of another" (as quoted in Hollis, 1995, p. 29). As Hollis points out, myth arises autonomously from the deep unconscious or from a phenomenological encounter with transcendent personal experience. According to Jung,

the primitive mentality does not *invent* myths, it

experiences them. Myths are original revelations of the preconscious psyche. . . . Many of these unconscious processes may be indirectly occasioned by consciousness, but never by conscious choice. Others appear to arise spontaneously, that is to say, from no discernible or demonstrable conscious cause. (as quoted in Hollis, pp. 29-30)

The Eternal Return and the Heroic Quest

The myth of the "Eternal Return: Sacrifice, Death, and Rebirth" embodies the cyclic quality of nature, the rhythm and return of human experience (Hollis, 1995, p. 54). This cycle is also seen in stories of the heroic quest.

The story of the tragic hero touches us because he or she exemplifies the dilemma in each of us. Fate wounds and surrounds, and from that intersection between fate and character history is generated. This history is both personal and collective, for often such a figure embodies the hopes and aspirations, as well as the shadow, of a whole people. (p. 55)

In embarking on the heroic journey,

the hero is always "called," although he or she may not initially understand this as a call or even wish to be called. Seldom is the way clear. Certainly it is never easy. The hero must persist, with the greatest obstacle being his or her own lethargy, fear, and longing for home. Sometimes the hero will receive critical aid from another. The path is strewn with various temptations—the devil of doubt, hope for an easier way, seductions of hedonism. (p. 57)

Hollis clearly explains the psychological meaning of the journey:

Often the hero of such stories sets out on an adventure in the world; sometimes the journey is internal as the hero descends into the depths of the unconscious. If the hero survives the descent—and typically many predecessors did not—and the battle with whatever monsters await in the depths, then he or she is able to undertake the ascent and be transformed. This transformation constitutes a death and rebirth experience. Who the person was, and what his or her conscious world was like, is no more. All is transformed.

Often these struggles have wounded the person. Wounds quicken consciousness and, as we recall from the mythology of the eternal return, are the quid pro quo for enlargement. Frequently there are tokens of this new state— a pot of gold, the hand of the beloved, a new homeland— but these are only the outward vestiges of a changed relationship of soul to cosmos.

As tokens of this change are irrelevant to the worth of the transformation of consciousness, such trophies need to be seen metaphorically. Any quest for the trophies themselves would be materialism, seeking the icon instead of the god, and losing the point of it all. While the journey of the hero may take the form of outer adventures, the goal is inner transformation.

The return is seldom back to the old land and never back to the old psychology. Such a return would obviate the journey and annihilate consciousness. Rather the return involves circling back at a higher level. Thus the in-forming image of the quest motif is not a linear movement once and for all time, but rather an evolutionary movement akin to a spiral. This voyage necessarily differentiates a person, develops a new being who may no longer be recognizable by the old tribe or the old values. The hero must bear the burden of loneliness and guilt, and, as Jung notes, must give something back. (pp. 65-74)

Through careful analysis and tracking of the autobiographical heuristic component of this study, along with the participant's interviews, one can follow the central Jungian and mythological concepts detailed by Hollis (1995) in his work, *Tracking the Gods: The Place of Myth in Modern Life*. To live through the descent to the Underworld and make one's way back to the Upperworld, to ascend, to come to life again after a period of emotional deadness is indeed living the modern-day myth of the hero's journey. It is living the myth of the "Eternal Return: Sacrifice, Death, and Rebirth" (p. 54) today in modern life and times, in ways that may appear deceptively simple and mundane but are nonetheless painful, dangerous, and infinitely difficult to combat and conquer; yet everyday, people are doing so as unsung, unrecognized, modern-day heroes. Their stories are a testament not only to their strength, courage, and resilience, but to that of the human race as a whole. For any individual trapped in the underground, not sure if there is a way out, these real-life, modern-day personal stories offer the hope and promise that there is a way back and that heroes do not just exist in ancient fables and fanciful story books. They walk among us every day.

The Transformative Power of Coming to Life Again
After a Period of Emotional Deadness

If it is true that the great myths and myth-making institutions sought to activate and channel the libido of the individual, then the erosion of such powerful guiding images acts as a psychological abandonment. So we are obliged to be even more conscious of our developmental task, since we must often undertake it in solitude and silence.

The "deadly longing for the abyss" that Jung speaks of is the grinning Gremlin Lethargy. The other one, Fear, is natural to the fragile human who works so hard to achieve a measure of security only to find that it is a trap, a stultification of the life force. To grow, to individuate, obliges us to reject that security and move into the unknown. Jung puts it dramatically:

The spirit of evil is fear, negation. . . . He is the spirit of regression, who threatens us with bondage to the mother and with dissolution and extinction in the unconscious....For the hero, fear is a challenge and a task, because only boldness can deliver from fear. And if the risk is not taken, the meaning of life is somehow violated, and the whole future is condemned to hopeless staleness, to a drab grey lit only by will-o'-the-wisps.

We are each obliged to suffer, to meditate upon, to incarnate, our unique experience of the cycle of sacrifice-death-rebirth, and, equally, to overthrow the gremlins of lethargy and fear to become that which nature so mysteriously offered. When we have taken on this unique yet absolute requirement that we become the protagonist in our own life drama, then we are living heroically. (Hollis, 1995, pp. 75-77)

All of the participants reported significant life-altering transformations from their experience of the descent and return. From having a sense of greater spirituality, connectedness, and gratitude to feelings of inner strength, being a living legacy, and knowing that one is a survivor, no one remained unscathed or unchanged. The transformation made deep, progressive, far-reaching, and long-lasting changes in all the participants who made the heroic journey.

Tales of Awakening

CHAPTER 6
SUMMARY AND CONCLUSIONS

This final chapter reviews the nature and findings of this research study, discusses the implications of the findings for the fields of depth and clinical psychology, offers suggestions for future research, and includes some final thoughts and experiences from this researcher.

Summary of the Nature and Structure of the Study

Through personal accounts, including an autobiographical heuristic component along with participant interviews, this study sought to explore the phenomenological experience of coming to life again after a period of emotional deadness. Though this particular theme has been broadly addressed throughout history and across cultures in multiple media such as archetype, literature, mythology, fairy tale, alchemy, religion, fable, and so on, it has it has faded in our current era.

The concept of descending to the Underworld, making the treacherous heroic journey, ascending to the Upperworld to return a changed being was neither prominent nor even present in the literature review conducted for this study in today's psychological databases. This concept appeared to be a construct of ancient times, stories of the Gods and Goddesses, and characters far removed from everyday human beings, yet as the researcher who chose this topic, or had this topic choose me, I knew this was not the case. The goal then, became giving voice to the modern day heroic warrior, the current Inannas and Persephones.

I was not interested in "depression" or "happiness" per se, but in the journey betwixt and between; the pivotal moments of transformation in and out of these states; and first-person, individual, phenomenological accounts of the lived experiences of essentially dying and coming back to life, of going to hell and surviving to return to tell the tale. People were eager to share their experiences in the hope it would help others believe there was a way back, when it seemed there was not and all was hopeless.

In this phenomenological study, five in-depth interviews were conducted, along with the inclusion of an autobiographical heuristic chapter. The interviews were with 5 participants who voluntarily self-identified as having come alive again after a period of emotional deadness. The interviews were approximately 1 hour in length. Two males and three females ranging in age from 33 to 47 years old participated. Including the author, 6 participants were contributed to the data collection.

After the participants interviews were transcribed, the informants were asked to review, verify, and make any changes to the interview transcriptions if needed. Once the transcriptions were accepted by the participants, they were analyzed using Giorgi's (1985) phenomenological method, consisting of identifying the natural meaning units in each interview, grouping these by theme, and verifying with the informants that the themes

Tales of Awakening

were in fact reflective of the experience. Next, the common themes of the experience were identified. From an analysis of these, a structural description of the experience of coming to life again after a period of emotional deadness was developed.

Summary of the Findings

Eight Common Themes

This researcher found eight common themes essential to the experience of coming back to life after a period of emotional deadness:

1. Major Trauma
2. Emotional Deadness
3. Crisis
4. Intervention
5. Painful Awakening
6. Taking Action
7. Sharing the Trauma/Telling the Story
8. New Life/New Identity

In addition to the common themes, a great variety of individual themes were presented that sometimes showed surprising variation from person to person and about the nature of the Underworld to Upperworld return.

Structural Description

Finally, from the common themes, this researcher developed the following structural description of the experience of coming to life again after a period of emotional deadness.

The experience of coming to life again after a period of emotional deadness, though somewhat variable for each individual who makes such a difficult journey, involves certain key themes or components which remain stable from participant to participant. The journey begins by entering the Underworld due to some form of great pain, loss, separation, betrayal, isolation, or exclusion. After suffering this type of major trauma, those who do make their way back develop or discover temporary coping mechanisms such as self-medicating or self-deprecation. Next, they encounter a turning point in the form of a crisis and an intervention, often in the form of another person entering the scene. This leads to a personal transformation of an awakening, frequently spiritual in nature, a sense of healing, and the taking of some kind of action. Ideally, in the Upperworld, individuals experience a sense of a new life and a new identity. This is often propelled by the act of sharing their trauma or telling their story to others.

Limitations of the Study

Unlike quantitative research, the qualitative method used in this study does not allow for the statistical generalization of the findings; however, Giorgi's (1985) phenomenological method of analysis, which was used to code the data, is systematic and general. The themes that were found common for the participants in this study may not be applicable to everyone who has had the experience of coming alive again after a period of emotional deadness, but they should be typical of the experience in general.

Implications of the Findings

Implications for Clinical Psychology

A primary implication for clinical psychology is the fact that the underworld journey is not, per se, a bad experience to be avoided. The current trend to medicalize, label, medicate, and consider difficult times of passage as disease states to be eradicated could learn from this study. Deeper changes are at work under the surface when one goes underground. If therapists are too uncomfortable to sit in the room with the emotionally dead, as many of them are, then the focus of therapy and treatment is on boosting them up before they are ready. The value of the Underworld journey, the heroic return, the alchemical opus, and individuation itself is then lost. No longer will those of us who experience this journey to the Underworld find our inner strength to realize we are warriors and survivors; no longer will there be modern-day epic quests.

Therapists who do not come from a depth perspective, though certainly having puzzle pieces of value to add to the treatment picture, can and should broaden their outlook to allow a place for the soul to speak, to process, and to be reborn. This may well prove difficult to do if one has not had a depth experience oneself.

This experience was previously well-documented and understood only through mythology, fairy tale, and religion. This study provided both autobiographical-heuristic and phenomenological participant interviews giving first-person accounts of the experience of coming back to life again after a period of emotional deadness. These accounts allowed for an in-depth examination of the experience, the gathering of salient common themes, and the construction of a structural description of the experience itself, all of which offer new information to both researchers and practicing therapists in the field.

Implications for Depth Psychology

This study contributes to the literature in depth psychology in the following meaningful ways.

Increased phenomenological understanding of the lived experience of coming to life again after a period of emotional deadness. First, this study used one of the primary research methods of depth psychology, the phenomenological method of investigation and data analysis, to further the field's understanding of the phenomena of coming to life again after a period of emotional deadness. The experience is akin to the alchemical process of turning base metal into the Philosopher's stone through a series of stages of cooking and processing until the final product is rendered.

Mythology is alive and well today. The stories gathered here, both autobiographical and interview, show poignantly that the central themes of archetypal psychology, mythology, alchemy, fairy tale, and so on, are being lived today as they were in the past. They have, however, been sublimated out of psyche, culture, and language, leaving those caught up in the mythic story no language to describe their experience, no way to make sense of what is happening to them, and no sense of belonging to a continuum of human experience that has been and always shall be. This study has given voice and structure to everyday heroic journeys and their archetypal figures, helping participants to understand that they did not suffer isolated persecutions. It has allowed them to become beacons to others who are making their way, giving purpose to their strife and success, like Persephone with her newfound role as Queen of the Dead.

Support for the role of depth psychological approaches to treatment. The current study lends credence to the unique role offered by the depth psychotherapy approaches to working with patients. Rather than focusing so specifically on a diagnostic label and a matching treatment plan dictated by a managed care insurance panel or a laboratory result, the patient is seen in a context. This context is the archetypal, alchemical, phenomenological context of coping with universal human issues, painful and individual as they may feel. By reflecting on the participant's interviews, the myths, the autobiographical heuristic component of the study, the fairy tales, and the alchemical descriptions which mirror Jung's individuation process, both therapists and patients can take heart in knowing that these situations, tragic as they are, always have been and always will be. Therapists who follow a depth approach are assisting and bearing witness to the difficult work of individuation and spiritual and emotional growth. Those who do the sacred work are not only reincarnating within themselves, but are truly continuing the archetypal work of living the myth forward.

Social and Cultural Implications

The social and cultural implications of this study could be very powerful. As the participants themselves stated repeatedly, they hoped that sharing their stories would offer help to those caught in the Underground, believing there was no way out. Their testimony could offer a glimmer of light to patients suffering from major depressive episodes, bereavement grief, posttraumatic stress-related issues, and shock and may dissuade those who feel lifeless and hopeless from committing self-harm or suicide.

Reading about real-life people who went through enormous pain and triumphed over tragedy and equating their experiences with larger-than-life mythic heroic figures could prove to be inspiring or to stimulate awakening in ways not previously seen.

Suggestions for Future Research

This study is just a tiny window into the lived experience of coming to life again after a period of emotional deadness. There is much to explore in this area, but for the sake of a particular study, the depth and scope of research necessarily must be limited. Closer investigations could be made into each of the four levels of the journey proposed here, that is, studies exclusively examining the phenomenological experiences of being in the Underworld or Emotionally Dead, having a Turning-Point moment, going through a Transformation phase, and being back in the Upperworld or emotionally alive once more.

Researchers could look for factors in terms of environmental triggers and internal characteristics that allow certain individuals to undergo this archetypal journey. Additionally, they might investigate what environmental and internal variables make some individuals less likely to confront such issues. It would be worth noting if participants' lives are truly better in some measurable way after undergoing the process of the Return, or if that claim is a coping or defense mechanism informants use in hindsight to alleviate further suffering for the psyche.

Future research could follow whether or not offering real-life stories of the Descent and Ascent, with and without associated mythological and literary accounts, is or is not of any benefit to patients currently in the Underworld, transitioning out of it, or even, in hindsight, from the Upperworld, and if so, how so. It could be determined when, where, and how best to employ the use of such materials in therapy, at what phase of treatment, and for how long. Finally, future research could note whether this type of material has any value as a self-help tool for the lay person.

Some Final Words on the Researcher's Experience

I was taught in my doctoral program that your dissertation topic will choose you; you will not choose your topic. There is a famous maxim, "Life is what happens while you are busy making other plans." To my not-so-great amusement, "If you want to make God laugh, start making plans" also comes to mind. I am not sure if that is actually a quote or just something I made up. Like any great endeavor that takes a relatively long chunk of time, say half a decade or so, things are bound to change along the way, and so it is that this process and this topic have been associated from the start with some extremely jarring change.

I was planning to write my doctoral dissertation on the topic of chronic pain and illness. I was rather abruptly blindsided by my 27-year-old fiancé's death. I apparently boarded the Ticket to Hell Ride at Disneyland without my knowledge and woke up after a long, strange time to find myself not the girl I had been before. I was seized with the knowledge of what I had to write about: coming alive again after a period of emotional deadness. I was utterly clueless that this was an archetypal life experience documented cross-culturally in myths, fairy tales, and all types of storytelling. I did know I had not seen or heard much about this experience in modern, everyday accounts, let alone mixed with the language I was feeling and hearing in my heart and soul: depth language. I had seen books about people who survived in the wilderness and who lived through being the victim of a crime, but nothing about surviving emotional deadness.

When my literature search failed to produce much, my committee directed me to the world of mythology, archetype, fairy tale, and alchemy for examples of my theme throughout history. I set about finding current, everyday representatives who had lived through the ancient death-rebirth cycle to share their stories. I shared my own.

Little did I know that this topic, of which I was so fond, was going to become my coyote for the next 7 years. I had barely returned to the Upperworld long enough to enjoy it before I became gravely ill and was thrown back into the Underworld, losing my friends, my family, my dearly beloved dogs, and quite literally, my actual life. This time, I was on the verge of physical death along with emotional death. It was during this entire time, from the moment my fiancé's death provoked the concept for my dissertation, until today, approximately 7 years later, that I struggled to stay alive and produce this work.

There were days where I literally could not function. There were days when I could not look at the dissertation. Reading, transcribing, and eliciting themes from the participants' interviews was deeply moving and touching yet also very sad. I was immensely honored that they would share such personal material with me for my study and that they were motivated to help others. I was continuously amazed at their courage, confidence, strength, and fighting spirit. It was always peculiar for me to read my own material. It was like reading about a third party. It still is. I was in awe of what that person lived through. I still am. I felt sad for her. I still do. I thought she was funny. She still is.

The process stretched on far longer than I ever imagined it would take, due to tiny roadblocks like my fiancé dying and me almost dying. I imagined I would never finish. I developed a full-fledged love-hate relationship with the dissertation. It became a living entity, an actual party known as "The Diss." It kept me from doing a lot of things, it was always around whether I wanted it to be or not, and people got really sick of hearing me talk about it. My running joke was that my tombstone would say "She was

Tales of Awakening

almost done" or "She almost finished." I often said either I was going to kill the Diss or it was going to kill me.

I mention all this because I had planned to write about this experience not only from the Upperworld, but more importantly, from *outside* the journey, as someone who had been there, done that, and was reporting on it in hindsight; but as Coyote would have it, the plan was for me somehow to live the experience again and write and report about it from the *inside*. No small feat, but I believe it was I who said that everything happens for a reason, there is a reason for everything that happens, and we are all exactly where we are supposed to be, experiencing what we are supposed to be experiencing, when we are experiencing it, even if it does not make sense right now.

REFERENCES

Abrams, J., & Zweig, C. (1991). Introduction: The shadow side of everyday life. In C. Zweig & J. Abrams (Eds.), *Meeting the shadow: The hidden power of the dark side of human nature* (pp. xvi-xxv). New York: Penguin.

Adams, T. (1995). *Angel of madness, creative muse: Suicide's voice and images.* Unpublished doctoral dissertation, Pacifica Graduate Institute, Carpinteria, CA.

The American heritage dictionary of the English language. (1973). New York: Houghton.

American Psychiatric Association, (2000). *Diagnostic and statistical manual of mental disorders* (4th ed., text revision). Washington, DC: Author.

Bolen, J. S. (1996). *Close to the bone: Life-threatening illness and the search for meaning.* New York: Touchstone.

Bonanno, G. A., & Kaltman, S. (1999). Toward an integrative perspective on bereavement. *Psychological Bulletin, 125,* 760-786. Washington DC: American Psychological Association.

Boss, P., & Couden, B. A. (2002). Ambiguous loss from chronic physical illness: Clinical interventions with individuals, couples, and families. *In Session: Psychotherapy in Practice, 58*(11), 1351-1360.

Bothamley, J. (2002). *Dictionary of theories: One stop to more than 5,000 theories.*
   Detroit: Visible Ink Press.

Campbell, J. (2008). *The hero with a thousand faces* (3rd ed.). Novato, CA: New World Library.

Chalquist, C. (2004). *What is depth psychology?* Retrieved April 1, 2008, from http:// www.tearsofllorona.com/depth.html

Chodron, P. (1997). *When things fall apart: Heart advice for difficult times.* Boston: Shambhala.

Creswell, J. (1998). *Qualitative inquiry and research design: Choosing among the five traditions.* Thousand Oaks, CA: Sage.

Dembski, W. (2006). *Alchemy and the emergence of complex systems.* Retrieved July 7, 2008, from http://www.leaderu.com/offices/dembski/docs/bd-alchemy.html

Elder, J. (2001). *The descent of Inanna: Magic is the art and science of changing consciousness at will.* Retrieved July 10, 2008, from http://www.jelder.com/ mythology/inanna/html

Fidel-Rice, A. (2002). *The alchemy of grief.* Unpublished doctoral dissertation, Pacifica Graduate Institute, Carpinteria, CA.

Flora, C. (2006). Therapy: The quick fix. Can therapy work in just a few sessions? *PsychologyToday.com.* Retrieved December 12, 2007, from http://health.msn. com/health-topics/depression/articlepage.aspx?cp-documentid=100136642

Flores, P. (1997). *Group psychotherapy with addicted populations: An integration of 12-step and psychodynamic therapy.* Binghamton, NY: Haworth Press.

Franz, M-L. von. (1980). *Alchemy: An introduction to the symbolism and the psychology.* Toronto, Canada: Inner City Books.

Giorgi, A. (1985). *Phenomenology and psychological research.* Pittsburgh, PA: Duquesne University Press.

Goodchild, V. (2001). *Eros and chaos: The sacred mysteries and dark shadows of love.* York Beach, ME: Nicolas-Hayes.

Grote, B. (2005). *The experience of feeling really understood in psychotherapy: A phenomenological study.* Unpublished doctoral dissertation, Pacifica Graduate Institute, Carpinteria, CA.

Henderson, J., & Oakes, M. (1963). *The wisdom of the serpent.* Princeton, NJ: Princeton University Press.

Hillman, J. (1983). *Healing fiction.* Woodstock, CT: Spring.

Hillman, J. (1997). *Suicide and the soul.* Putnam, CT: Spring.

Hollis, J. (1995). *Tracking the gods: The place of myth in modern life.* Toronto, ON, Canada: Inner City Books.

Hyde, L. (1998). *Trickster makes this world: Mischief, myth, and art.* New York:
Farrar.

Jung, C. G. (1967). The dual mother. In H. Read, M. Fordham, G.

Adler, & W. McGuire (Eds.), *The collected works of C. G. Jung* (R. F. C. Hull, Trans.) (2ⁿᵈ. ed., Vol. 5ii, pp. 306-393). Princeton, NJ: Princeton University Press. (Original work published 1952)

Jung, C. G. (1968). Religious ideas in alchemy. In H. Read, M. Fordham, G. Adler, & W. McGuire (Eds.), *The collected works of C. G. Jung* (R. F. C. Hull, Trans.) (2ⁿᵈ. ed., Vol. 12, pp. 225-471). Princeton, NJ: Princeton University Press. (Original work published 1937)

Kiehl, J. (2005). *The phenomenological experience of depression.* Retrieved April 7, 2008, from http://www.cgjungpage.org/index.php?option=com

Lock, H. (2002). *Transformations of the trickster.* Retrieved April 9, 2008, from http://www.southerncrossreview.org/18/trickster.htm

Macary, M. (2005, October 31). Blog message. Retrieved July 10, 2009, from http://www.mythandculture.com/weblog/2005/10/imagineseries. msnw?action=get_message&mview=1&ID_Message=10627

Martin, M. P. (1996). *Illness as transformation: A phenomenological study of women's experience of breast cancer.* Unpublished doctoral dissertation, Pacifica Graduate Institute, Carpinteria, CA.

Matsakis, A. (2008). *Depression: Friend or foe?* Retrieved February 10, 2010, from http://searchwarp.com/swa299930.htm

Moustakas, C. (1994). *Phenomenological research methods.*

Thousand Oaks, CA:
    Sage.

The New York Association for Analytical Psychology (2008). Retrieved April 13, 2008, from http://www.nyaap.org/index.php/id/1

Orbis, H. (2007). *Samhain 2007: Persephone and the underworld.* Retrieved December 10, 2007, from http://www.typepad.com/services/trackback/6a00d83452ff0d69 e200e54f7 fed758833

Romanyshyn, R. (1999). *The soul in grief: Love, death, and transformation.* Berkeley, CA: North Atlantic Books.

Romanyshyn, R. (2001). *Mirror and metaphor: Images and stories of psychological life.* Pittsburgh, PA: Trivium.

Rutzky, J. (1998). *Coyote speaks: Psychotherapy with alcoholics and addicts.* Lanham, MD: Aronson.

Schreiber, R. (1998). Clueing in: A guide to solving the puzzle of self for women recovering from depression. *Health Care for Women International, 19*(4), 269-289.

Seifert, T. (1986). *Snow White: Life almost lost.* Wilmette, IL: Chiron.

Sharp, D. (1991). *Jung lexicon: A primer of terms and concepts.* Retrieved July 10, 2007, from http://www.cgjungpage.org/index.php?option=com_content&tas k=view&id =869&Itemid=41

Smith, L. E. (1990). *Rape and revelation: The descent to the underworld in modernism.* Lanham, MD: University Press of America.

Spector, B. (2005). Rituals of grief.
Retrieved July 20, 2008, from http://www. headlinemuse.com/Culture/ritualsofgrief.htm

Strong, L. (2000). *The myth of Persephone: Greek goddess of the underworld.* Retrieved July 15, 2007, from http://www.mythicarts.com/writing/Persephone.htm

United Studios of Self Defense, Inc. (1990). *Student manual.* USA: Author.

Wolkstein, D., & Kramer, N. (1983). *Inanna, queen of heaven and earth: Her stories and hymns.* New York: Harper.

Woodman, M. (2000). *Bone: Dying into life, a journal of wisdom, strength, and healing.* New York: Penguin Books. Retrieved December 12, 2007, from http://www. alsirat.com/city.html

Worth, P. (1996). Inanna: Goddess of transformative relationships. *Sage Woman, 34,* 38.

Appendix A

Informed Consent Form

Title of the Study: *"Tales of Awakening: A phenomenological study of the lived experience of coming to life again after a period of emotional deadness."*

1.   I agree to be interviewed by Heidi Elowitch on the topic of my experience of coming alive again after a period of emotional deadness. I understand that Heidi will ask me to talk about and describe a time (or times) in my life when I experienced a sense of coming to life again after a period of feeling emotionally dead.

2.   Upon completion of a brief information form, I will be interviewed and give a response that is the length of my choosing. After my response is transcribed, I will receive a copy and complete a short telephone interview in which I will be asked if I have any comments or clarifications. In addition, Heidi will share with me the themes that emerged from my interview and I will be able to comment on them. I understand that all of the interview materials will be kept confidential.

3.   The purpose of this study is to investigate the lived experience of coming alive again after a period of emotional deadness.

4.   I understand that it is possible that the interview

may trigger strong emotions and/or memories, both positive and negative, which may cause psychological stress or discomfort. I understand that I may temporarily suspend or voluntarily discontinue my involvement in the process at any time. If needed, Heidi will provide me with psychotherapy referrals which will be my responsibility to cover the cost of. I understand that a pseudonym will be provided to insure my confidentiality and that my interview response will only be used by the researcher, Heidi Elowitch, and her dissertation committee for data analysis.

5.   I understand that this study is of a research nature and may be of no direct benefit to me. My interview material will be used to further psychotherapists' understanding of the experience of coming alive again after a period of emotional deadness.

6.   Information pertaining to this study, and my contribution to it, was discussed with me by Heidi Elowitch. I am aware that I may contact her at anytime by calling (805) 732-9446.

7.   Participation in this study is voluntary. I may decide not to enter the study or to withdraw from it. I may do this at any time with no adverse consequences. I also understand that the researcher may have to drop me from the study for unforeseen reasons.

8.   I am not receiving any monetary compensation for being a part of this study.

Heidi Elowitch (Taylor)

Appendix B
Instructions to Participants

1. Your audio taped response to the interview question may take place at a time and location convenient to you, and may be of any length you feel necessary to provide your full and complete response.

2. The interview will be transcribed by the researcher. Your confidentiality will be respected at all times.

3. You will be asked to describe an experience or experiences in which you felt as if you came back to life after a period of emotional deadness and returned to a sense of being alive once more, with particular focus on the circumstances surrounding the transformation between the two stages. You are encouraged to describe the experience in as much detail and specificity as possible in relation to all aspects which feel relevant and important to you.

4. While discussing your experience, intense or painful memories or emotions may arise. You may feel upset, sad, or otherwise disturbed by these psychological reactions. You are free to take a break and resume at your discretion,

as well as to discontinue participation entirely at any point in the study. If you feel the need to obtain therapy or related services, referrals will be provided.

5. Following the review of your personal interview, you will have a follow-up interview with the researcher and asked if any comments or clarification are needed. You will be informed about the psychological themes the researcher has obtained from your interview response and given the opportunity to comment on them. You will be provided with a copy of your transcribed interview.

Appendix C

Participant Recruitment Flyer

"Tales of Awakening: A phenomenological study of the lived experience of coming to life again after a period of emotional deadness."

If you are interested in sharing your experience/s of awakening from a period of emotional deadness, please consider the following study:

I am looking for individuals who feel they have had the experience of coming back to life again after a period of emotional deadness. For the purpose of this study this is being defined as the transitive phase between feeling numb and cut off from the world, normally after some type of traumatic event or loss, to somehow reconnecting with the world and feeling alive once more. I would like participants to share their personal account in an audio-taped interview of such an experience or experiences in their lives. My research goal is to encourage the therapeutic community's understanding of this process and possibly discover new ways to facilitate it. Your identity will be kept confidential in this study.

I am a doctoral student in Clinical Psychology at Pacifica Graduate Institute in Santa Barbara, California. I reside in Thousand Oaks, California. If you are interested in participating, please contact me at any time: Heidi M. Elowitch, M.S., (805) 732-9446, h.gemini1@verizon. Thank you for your interest.

Tales of Awakening

Appendix D

Participant Information Form

Name_____

Address_____

Phone

W/H/C_____

Age_____

Occupation_____

Appendix E

Table E1

Common Elements Participants Mentioned Describing the Underworld

---

Complete emptiness
Extreme terror
Unbearable suffering
Feeling unknown
Feeling alone
Feeling estranged
Feeling rejected
Feeling excluded
Feeling withdrawn
Feeling anhedonic
Feeling annihilated
Feeling emotionally broken down
Filled with self-doubt
Self-blame
Recipients of numerous types of abuse
Loss of eros
Lowered self-esteem
Self-injurious behavior
Lost opportunities
Stunned disbelief
Desperate bargaining
Utter hopelessness
Great pain
Tragic losses
Separations
Isolation
Exclusion
Multiple betrayals

Tales of Awakening

Suicidal/death thoughts
Emotional deadness
Coping mechanisms
Self-deprecation
Self-medicating

Appendix F

Table F1

Common Elements Participants Mentioned Describing the Turning Point

---

Catastrophe
Opportunity
New words
New actions
New person
Perspective shift

Tales of Awakening

Appendix G

Table G1

Common Elements Participants Mentioned Describing the Transformation

---

New/greater spiritual connections
Painful awakening
Sense of movement/breakthrough to a new dimension
Sharing the trauma
Telling the story to others
Receiving support
Sense of healing
Taking action on multiple levels: social, physical, legal, dietary, educational, cognitive, medical, psychological, and emotional
Feelings of acceptance, forgiveness, gratitude, and wholeness.

Appendix H

Table H1

Common Elements Participants Mentioned Describing the Upperworld

---

Felt blessed
Empowered
Hopeful
Blissful
Grateful
Forgiving
Wise
Growth time
Destiny
Self-discovery
Share recovery
Give help
Made sense of their experience and suffering if it could be used to ease the suffering of others and give them guidance and hope

---

Tales of Awakening

Appendix I

Table I1

Common Elements Mentioned Describing the Journey

Levels of the Journey	Descriptive elements
The Underworld	Weighty
	Dark
	Dry
	Low
	Too real to escape from in fantasy
The Turning Point	"Knight in Shining Armor" individual who assisted in their intervention
The Transformation	"Awakening to the universal experience"
The Upperworld	Being a survivor
	Being a living legacy for a loved one who had died
	Experiencing self-love for the first time

Heidi Elowitch (Taylor)

Appendix J

Table J1
_____

Common "Do's and Don'ts" for Those in the Sphere of a Heroic Journeyer
_____

Do: Accept and normalize a range of feelings and emotions normally viewed as negative and the object of rapid eradication

Accept that depression, shock, posttraumatic stress, and complicated bereavement will heal slowly and gradually

Offer personal or other sources showing that return and recovery are possible
Let individuals tell their story as much as they need to

Don't: Blame

Be afraid

Judge

Expect things to be "normal"

Overreact to depressive or suicidal statements

Struggle over feelings or coping mechanisms

Underestimate recovery time

About the Author

Heidi Taylor, PhD is a therapist and Supervised Visitation Monitor who lives with her 3 precious dogs and 3 roommates in Southern California. It took her 5 years to write this labor of love and she hopes it will be helpful to others who are in the midst of grief or depression, as a guide to find their way back to life.

www.ingramcontent.com/pod-product-compliance
Lightning Source LLC
Chambersburg PA
CBHW072039280526
45788CB00006B/2116